SPOTLIGHT

COLUMBIA RIVER GORGE

ERICKA CHICKOWSKI

Contents

COLUMBIA RIVER GORGE

COLUMBIA RIVER GORGE AND WINE COUNTRY

Follow the course of the mighty Columbia River from Vancouver eastward and you'll experience a parade of photogenic panoramas. From the sheer basalt cliffs diving into the river's depths along the Columbia Gorge to the windswept wheat hillocks of Walla Walla to the shady apple orchards of Yakima, the region is the stuff of postcards.

It's not just a feast for the eyes, either: This is Washington wine country. Resting at the same latitude as the famed French wine chateaus of Bordeaux and Burgundy, central Washington's distinct landscapes are bound together in the pursuit of perfecting reds and whites. Over the last decade, the state has seen an explosion in wineries—from slightly over 100 in 1997 to more than 500 now. Most of those new growers and winemakers have set up shop in central Washington, home of seven of the eight official wine appellations in Washington.

A day's drive can put you in position to walk the rows at scenic vineyards and chat up winemakers in their cozy tasting rooms. Wine country wanderers will also find artisan cheeses, freshly picked fruits, and other culinary delights dished up in the hidden countryside cafés and bistros that have sprung up from the region's viticultural boom. And you needn't worry about the scale after your gastronomic excess: The region offers plenty of outdoor activities that will make a four-course meal and a bottle of wine seem well justified by day's end.

Cyclists can spin on serpentine bands of blacktop winding through the country past historic train depots and scenically dilapidated barns.

HIGHLIGHTS

◖ **Vancouver National Historic Reserve:** History buffs will be in heaven here, exploring a reconstructed Hudson's Bay Company fort, turn-of-the-20th-century barracks, and a historic airfield (page 12).

◖ **Beacon Rock State Park:** Lewis and Clark spotted this gigantic volcanic rock on their journey west. Climb to the top of the rock for the best view of the Gorge (page 21).

◖ **Columbia Hills State Park:** With pretty views, rock climbing, and fishing galore, this

park is best known for its amazing collection of petroglyphs and pictographs (page 31).

◖ **Maryhill Museum of Art:** Dubbed "Castle Nowhere," this remote museum is remarkable for its collections of Rodin sculptures and chess sets (page 33).

◖ **Gorge Waterfalls:** Set on the south side of the Gorge, the plunging waterfalls along the Historic Columbia River Highway are some of the most beautiful in the United States (page 41).

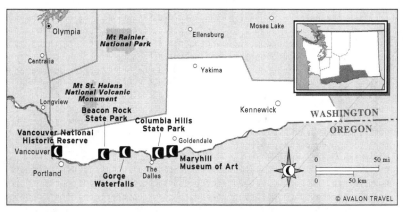

LOOK FOR ◖ TO FIND RECOMMENDED SIGHTS, ACTIVITIES, DINING, AND LODGING.

Hikers and equestrians can scramble through rugged multiuse trails in ponderosa stands, desert wildflowers, and sylvan canyons. And watersports lovers will be in heaven—temperatures soar on the dry eastern side of the Cascades, making the prospect of a good drenching more than appealing. Experience the wind-whipped excitement of kiteboarding or windsurfing the Columbia River. Or enjoy a lazy afternoon tubing or fly-fishing its tributaries.

So slip on your driving gloves and prepare to hit the road. Even the most remote

outposts along the Gorge and the rest of central Washington's country roads are well worth the trip.

In 1986, President Ronald Reagan signed into law a measure that established the **Columbia River Gorge National Scenic Area,** encompassing 292,000 acres on both sides of the river from Washougal to Maryhill. The national scenic area is managed jointly by the U.S. Forest Service, the states of Washington and Oregon, and six local counties across both states. Headquarters for the scenic area are in

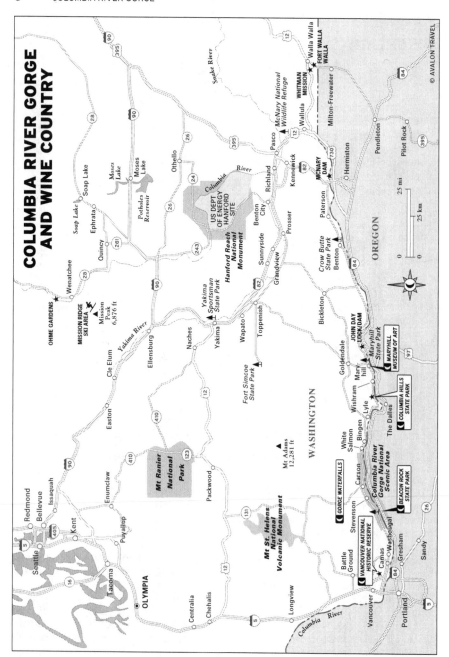

COLUMBIA RIVER GORGE
AND WINE COUNTRY

© AVALON TRAVEL

Hood River, Oregon; call 541/386-2333 for details.

A $5 National Forest Recreation Day Pass is required for parking at all Forest Service trailheads in the scenic area. Or pick up an annual Northwest Forest Pass ($30) that is valid for most national forest trailheads in Washington and Oregon. Get one from most local sporting-goods stores, any Forest Service office (800/270-7504), or at www.fs.fed.us/passespermits.

HISTORY

In 1792, American trading captain Robert Gray discovered the great Columbia River on his journey to become the first American to sail around the world. Gray claimed the river and its huge drainage area for the United States, naming the river after his ship, the *Columbia Rediviva* (Columbus Lives Again). After Gray's discovery, Vancouver sent William Broughton out to explore the upriver territory for England; Broughton asserted that Gray hadn't found the true channel and claimed the river for His Royal Majesty, the King. After Broughton's claim, the United States and Great Britain were unable to come to terms on the ownership of Oregon Country, a fur- and lumber-rich land that included the Northwest Coast of North America. In 1818, the two powers agreed to share the land until a long-term arrangement could be reached, but seven years later the British-owned Hudson's Bay Company moved its headquarters from Fort George, at the mouth of the Columbia, to Fort Vancouver, 100 miles inland, in hopes of solidifying the British claim to the region.

Fort Vancouver became the Pacific Northwest's commercial and cultural center for fur trading from Utah to Hawaii; shops, fields, pastures, and mills made the fort a self-sufficient, bustling pioneer community. The most famous Columbia River explorers were Meriwether Lewis and William Clark. Northwesterners won't be surprised to hear that Lewis and Clark recorded 31 consecutive days of rain during their visit to the region! The region's historic brush with the Corps

of Discovery piqued American interest in what was then called "Oregon Country." The floodgates opened in 1843, when the Applegate Wagon Train, the largest wagon train ever assembled anywhere, left Independence, Missouri. Under the leadership of Dr. Marcus Whitman and guided by mountain man Bill Sublette, the pioneers made it all the way to the Columbia and Willamette Rivers by September of that year. It had taken six long months to travel the 2,000 miles, but they had shown that the "Oregon Trail" route was feasible. Thousands of Americans seeking open vistas and economic opportunity would follow in the next two decades. The march west along the Oregon Trail is regarded as the greatest peacetime migration in America's history.

The Columbia River Gorge lay near the end of the journey for emigrants heading west and posed the last major obstacle along the way. The narrow confines of the gorge forced them to dismantle their wagons and load them onto log rafts to float down the river as far as the Cascades, which they portaged before continuing by raft to the area of present-day Portland. Treacherous rapids, strong currents, and high winds caused the deaths of many people almost within sight of the promised land. Completion of the Barlow Road in 1846—a toll route that avoided the gorge by heading south around the south shoulder of Mount Hood—provided a safer alternative to the Willamette Valley. It cost pioneers an exorbitant $5 a wagon and $0.10 a head for livestock to use the road.

These droves of pioneering Americans would happily pay the fee, though, as they were drawn to Oregon's fertile Willamette Valley farmland, a migration that eventually led to the division of the territory along the 49th parallel in 1846—a boundary that put Britain's Fort Vancouver squarely on American soil. By 1860 all of Fort Vancouver was in the hands of the U.S. Army. Decay and fire had destroyed all of the remaining structures by 1866. The Army constructed new buildings on the slope behind the fort at **Vancouver Barracks,** including officers' quarters, barracks and other facilities.

CLIMATE

The scenery along the route blends the green forested hills of the western section into the dry basaltic and barren hills of the eastern half. In a distance of just 40 miles—from Cascade Locks to The Dalles—average annual rainfall changes by 40 inches! The gorge has its own climate, and temperature extremes on the east side range from zero or less in winter to 110°F of dry heat in summer. It isn't unusual to descend into the Gorge and into a gale because this narrow gap is the only place weather systems can push through the towering mountains. Sometimes in the winter a sudden arctic blast comes down the Gorge to create an ice storm, which, around these parts, they call a "silver thaw."

PLANNING YOUR TIME

This stretch of the Columbia River is treasured by residents of both Washington and Oregon. No matter the season, no matter the weather conditions, the Gorge is always beautiful. You can choose your pace: I-84 roars along the Oregon side of the Gorge at river level, blasting through the rocky hills through a number of tunnels. On the Washington side, things are a little more relaxed. A cross between country road and highway gently follows the contours of the land and the bends of the river. On the western stretch, the Lewis and Clark Highway (State Route 14) winds through maple and Douglas fir forests punctuated by stunning vistas into the river valley far below.

The gorge between I-5 and Highway 97 is heavily traveled on both sides of the river, but the area from Highway 97 at Maryhill Museum east to Paterson is the less so, so expect fewer services. The descriptions in this chapter follow the Washington side of the river from Vancouver to McNary Dam, where the highway heads away from the river and north to the Tri-Cities area, and on the Oregon side from Troutdale to The Dalles.

Crossing the Columbia

Obviously, in a region centered around a dramatic river gorge, the placement of bridge

The Columbia River Gorge is a bi-state region enjoyed best from both Washington and Oregon.

© ERICKA CHICKOWSKI

THE BRIDGE OF THE GODS

The Klickitat, Yakima, and Warm Springs people of the Pacific Northwest all share a legend describing the creation and destruction of a massive stone bridge spanning the Columbia River between Skamania County and Cascade Locks, Oregon. According to the Klickitat version, two great chiefs, Klickitat and Wy'East, were given rich new lands by the Great Spirit, their respective lands separated by the Columbia. As a symbol of peace, the Great Spirit built an enormous bridge across the river, connecting the two territories. Unfortunately, the two groups took to fighting, and in the ensuing chaos, the enormous bridge was destroyed.

It's believed that the legend refers to a historical event – roughly 500 years ago, a powerful landslide was said to have blocked the Columbia River until the water flow eroded all but a slender bridge that crossed the river. Eventually, that bridge collapsed, but the rocks from the bridge have come to form the Columbia Rapids. Today, the modern steel-and-concrete Bridge of the Gods spans the river close to where the legendary bridge was thought to have been. In order to cross, you no longer have to contend with Loo-Wit, the appointed guardian of the bridge, but you will have to pay a buck in tolls.

crossings will play an important part in your trip planning. From the greater Portland/Vancouver region to the eastern edge of the National Scenic Area at Maryhill, you'll find six Columbia River bridges crisscrossing the Washington and Oregon state line. Two of the biggest run from Vancouver into Portland via I-5 and I-205, with the former rolling into downtown Portland and the latter further east near the Portland International Airport.

The next crossing isn't for another 35 miles further east. There, between Cascade Locks, Oregon, and the outskirts of Stevenson, Washington, the Bridge of the Gods runs over a narrow Columbia River passage, so named for an ancient land bridge that once formed here from a massive rock slide. The bridge costs $1 to pass each way. It is also, interestingly, the route Pacific Crest Trail hikers take to hike their way up the Washington section of the trail. Just east of the Bonneville Dam and west of Stevenson's nicer lodging, plus several miles east of Oregon's most accessible Gorge waterfalls, this link provides a nice means to connect shorter loops on the "wet"western portion of the Gorge byways.

A little over 20 miles past that, the Hood River Bridge connects Hood River, Ore. with White Salmon, Washington. This river crossing gives Gorge travelers the ability to stay in the nicer accommodations in Hood River while still being able to pop over to enjoy the rafting and fishing on the White Salmon River and enjoy the wildflower-studded trails of Washington in this section of the Gorge. Over 20 miles east of that The Dalles Bridge provides a vital link between the largest city within the National Scenic Area and the windswept Columbia Hills area of Washington. Many campers who stay at Washington's Columbia Hills State Park cap off their trip with a meal in The Dalles.

The last bridge within the Gorge's designated scenic area is an additional 20 miles east. The Sam Hill Memorial Bridge crosses the Columbia to connect Maryhill, Washington, to Biggs Junction, Oregon, and offers the opportunity to take the grand loop of all of the Gorge from either side of the river. If you were to start in Vancouver, drive east through Maryhill and Biggs Junction and then back west through Portland and Vancouver, the total drive time would equal about 4.5 hours straight through.

Vancouver

Situated in the crook of the elbow bend in the Lower Columbia River, Vancouver serves as a gateway to the Columbia Gorge, Mount St. Helens, and Portland just across the river. The unique riverside geography allows Vancouver to hang on to its slow-paced charm in spite of its inclusion in the metropolitan Portland scene, giving visitors a healthy blend between big city convenience and small-town relaxation. Much of the city's appeal is drawn from its colorful history, which is vividly illustrated at the town's premier attraction, the Vancouver National Historic Reserve.

SIGHTS
◖ Vancouver National Historic Reserve

No trip to Vancouver would be complete without an excursion to the Vancouver National Historic Reserve (from I-5 take E. Mill Plain Blvd. and turn left at Fort Vancouver Way), a trove of history and scenery that unfolds over hundreds of acres. Curious travelers will stumble

Fort Vancouver's recreated stockade

upon a reconstructed Hudson's Bay trading post, the only complete row of restored 19th-century officers' homes in the nation, and one of the oldest operating airfields in the country.

FORT VANCOUVER NATIONAL HISTORIC SITE

In this scenic park, the visitor will find accurate reconstructions of 6 of the 27 buildings the Hudson's Bay Company built here in 1845 to protect its fur-trapping interests. Surrounded by a tall wooden stockade and guarded by a three-story tower once armed with eight three-pound cannons, it's easy to get wrapped up in the history of the area.

Other reconstructed buildings include a blacksmith's shop, bakery, Native American trade shop, storage house, and the elegant residence of Dr. John McLoughlin, the chief factor. Although McLoughlin had been charged with keeping the American traders out of the market, he realized that their participation was far more practical. He later became an American citizen, moved to Oregon City, and is now hailed as the "Father of Oregon."

Historic Fort Vancouver (360/816-6230, 360/816-6200 for recorded info, www.nps .gov/fova, 9 A.M.–5 P.M. Mon.–Sat., $3 adults, kids under 15 free) offers a tour with a visit to the fully restored home of John McLoughlin, along with a visit to the working blacksmith shop where you will learn how the Hudson's Bay Company produced beaver traps and other goods. Today the shop is used to train apprentices to create iron pieces for National Park Service historic facilities across the nation. Also of interest during the tour are the living history activities that take place all summer. The fort's period gardens are interesting to view, and gardeners will be happy to tell you of the crops that were—and are—grown here.

A block north of the fort is the **visitors center** (1511 East Evergreen Blvd., same hours as the fort), where you can watch a 15-minute orientation video and view displays on

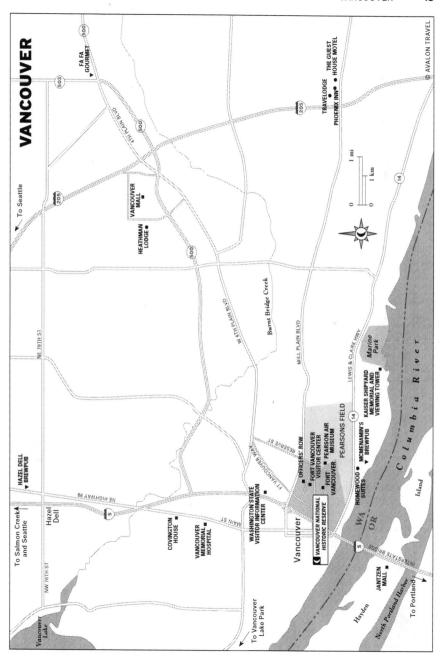

VANCOUVER

To Seattle

FA FA GOURMET

TRAVELODGE
PHOENIX INN
THE GUEST HOUSE MOTEL

AVALON TRAVEL

VANCOUVER MALL

HEATHMAN LODGE

Burnt Bridge Creek

W 4TH PLAIN BLVD

NE 78TH ST

1 mi
1 km

Columbia River

MILL PLAIN BLVD

LEWIS & CLARK HWY

Marine Park

KAISER SHIPYARD MEMORIAL AND VIEWING TOWER

NE HIGHWAY 99

HAZEL DELL BREWPUB

To Salmon Creek and Seattle

Hazel Dell

NW 78TH ST

Vancouver Lake

COVINGTON HOUSE

VANCOUVER MEMORIAL HOSPITAL

MAIN ST

WASHINGTON STATE VISITOR INFORMATION CENTER

FT VANCOUVER WAY

RESERVE ST

OFFICERS' ROW
FORT VANCOUVER VISITOR CENTER
FORT VANCOUVER
PEARSON AIR MUSEUM

PEARSONS FIELD

Vancouver

VANCOUVER NATIONAL HISTORIC RESERVE

HOMEWOOD SUITES
McMENAMIN'S BREWPUB

WA
OR

To Vancouver Lake Park

Hayden

JANTZEN MALL

INTERSTATE BRIDGE

North Portland Harbor

Island

To Portland

the fort along with artifacts found during the excavations.

VANCOUVER BARRACKS

Established in 1849 after the Whitman Massacre in Walla Walla, Vancouver Barracks played an important role in the U.S. Army for over a century. It was the central command post during the Northwest Indian Wars, and it was a mobilization center during the Spanish-American War and both World Wars. The site was continuously occupied by the Army and National Guard until 2011, when it was turned over to the National Park Service. It is now available to tour under its new name, Fort Vancouver National Historic Site. Take a stroll down the sun-speckled, tree-lined Barnes Street and McClellan and Hatheway Roads to get a close look at the picturesque brick structures built around the turn of the 20th century.

OFFICERS' ROW

The only complete row of restored Army officers' homes in the nation is at Vancouver's Officers' Row National Historic District. The homes occupy one side of a tree-shaded street and are now used by local businesses; opposite is spacious **Central Park**—a favorite place for locals to relax on a sunny day. Find here an old Army cemetery with the graves of around 1,400 soldiers, including four Medal of Honor recipients.

The two most famous buildings on Officers' Row are houses named for General George C. Marshall and President Ulysses S. Grant. The **Marshall House** (1313 Officers' Row, 360/693-3103, 9 A.M.–5 P.M. Mon.–Fri., and on select Saturdays) is open for free tours and has videotapes describing the fort and Officers' Row. The building is very popular for weddings and other events, so it is often closed to the public on weekends. Named for the man who authored the famous post-WWII Marshall Plan, it was George C. Marshall's home during his time as commanding officer at Vancouver Barracks, 1936–1938.

Built in 1849, **The Grant House** is the oldest remaining building on Officer's Row.

VANCOUVER, USA

The name, honoring Capt. George Vancouver, who explored the Columbia River in 1792, came from the Hudson's Bay post named Fort Vancouver. While the city was still part of the Oregon Territory, the Oregon Territorial Legislature named it Columbia City. However, in 1855, the legislature changed it back to its original name, creating a situation that will always cause confusion. Locals point out that Vancouver, British Columbia, is a Johnny-come-lately city and if any name should be changed, it should be the Canadian one. That prospect is doubtful. To help avoid confusion, the city is often referred to as Vancouver, USA, or specifically as Vancouver, Washington.

This stately home was built as the commanding officer's residence and is now home to **The Restaurant at Historic Reserve** (360/906-1101). While President Grant never actually lived in the house, he was a frequent visitor during his time as the post's quartermaster in the 1850s.

PEARSON AIRFIELD

Ever wanted to strap into a genuine flight simulator? The **Pearson Air Museum** (1115 E. 5th St., 360/694-7026, www.pearsonairmuseum.org, 10 A.M.–5 P.M. Wed.–Sat., $7 adults, $5 seniors and active duty military with ID, $3 ages 6–12, free for kids under age 6) offers you the chance. The museum also displays dozens of aircraft and memorabilia from all periods in aviation history. The adjacent Pearson Airfield is one of the oldest operating fields in the nation; its first landing was a dirigible that floated over from Portland in 1905, and the first plane arrived seven years later. This was also where the Russian transpolar flight ended in 1937.

Ridgefield National Wildlife Refuge

About half an hour north of Vancouver, nature lovers will have ample opportunity to explore fields, woodlands, and wetlands at Ridgefield National Wildlife Refuge (1071 S. Hillhurst

Rd., 360/887-4106, www.fws.gov/ridgefield refuges), which fans over 5,150 acres around the marshy lower Columbia River. Bring your binoculars in winter, when up to 10,000 geese and 40,000 ducks land here. Hiking and fishing are permitted—the two-mile **Oaks to Wetlands Wildlife Trail** is popular with all ages. Parts of the refuge are closed October–mid-April.

Clark County Historical Museum

The Clark County Historical Museum (1511 Main St., 360/993-5679, http://cchmuseum.org, 11 A.M.–4 P.M. Tues.–Sat., $4 adults, $3 students and seniors, $2 children 6–18, $10 for a family of four, free for historical society members and children under 5) hosts a changing lineup of exhibits related to Clark County History.

St. James Church

Be sure to drive by the St. James Church (12th and Washington Sts.). Built in 1885, this was the first Gothic Revival-style church in Washington and is home to the state's longest-standing Catholic congregation.

Parks

Marine Park occupies the site of the Kaiser Shipyards, where "Rosie the Riveter" hurriedly constructed more than 140 ships during World War II before the facilities were decommissioned and dismantled. Today you can climb a three-story riverside tower next to Kaiser Center for dramatic views of Vancouver and Portland. Also in the park is the new **Water Resources Education Center** (4600 SE Columbia Way, 360/696-8478, 9 A.M.–5 P.M. Mon.–Sat., free). The center houses hands-on exhibits, a video theater, and a 350-gallon aquarium filled with Columbia River creatures. Not far away is the **Chkalov Monument,** commemorating the Soviet transpolar flight of 1937, when three Russian aviators were the first to cross over the north pole and into America.

Old Apple Tree Park, along the river just east of I-5, honors what is believed to be the oldest apple tree in the Northwest. The tree was planted in 1826 and still bears small green apples each summer.

Shady **Esther Short Park** (W. 6th and Esther) contains the historic Slocum House Theater, along with a Victorian rose garden, playground, and a monument to pioneer women. The site is a popular one for festivals and concerts throughout the summer.

ENTERTAINMENT AND EVENTS

Nightlife

Enjoy the Columbia River view from **Beaches Restaurant & Bar** (1919 SE Columbia River Dr., 360/699-1592, www.beachesrestaurant andbar.com, 11 A.M.–9 P.M. Sun.–Mon., 11 A.M.–10 P.M. Tues.–Sat., bar open until 2 A.M.), a fun place with tasty appetizers, a diverse menu, and a hopping bar. Also facing the river is **Who-Song and Larry's Cantina** (111 E. Columbia Way, 360/695-1198, 11 A.M.–10 P.M. Sun.–Thurs., 11 A.M.–11 P.M. Fri.–Sat., bar open until 2 A.M.), where the singing waiters are a local phenomenon.

The Arts

Tired of living in Portland's shadow, proud Vancouverites have worked hard to establish a lively arts and entertainment scene of their own. Skip the bridge, and check out some of these local venues.

Listed on the National Register of Historic Homes, the 60-seat **Slocum House Theater** (360/696-2497, www.slocumhouse.com) was built in 1867. The theater stages productions year-round.

Music lovers need not venture south to enjoy a quality performance. The unique **Vancouver Symphony Orchestra** (360/735-7278, www .vancouversymphony.org) attracts talented local musicians and a roster of traveling professionals to its full season of classical performances. Its venue, Skyview Concert Hall (1300 NW 139th St.), is wonderfully intimate and acoustically striking. The season runs September–May annually.

The city's well-attended **Six to Sunset** (360/619-1111, www.cityofvancouver.us, free) concert series in central Esther Short Park sets out to offer something for everyone. These weekly summertime concerts range from orchestral music to Beatles cover bands to contemporary rock. Food vendors and blanket seating complete the town carnival atmosphere.

Festivals and Events

Don't miss the annual **Vancouver Rodeo** (360/896-6654, www.vancouverrodeo.com), a four-day benefit show taking place around the 4th of July. Look for bull-riding, dances, and even pony rides for the little 'uns. Also in summer, the annual **Fort Vancouver Brigade Encampment** fills the fort with trappers and traders dressed in 1840 period costumes. There are tepees, baking and cooking demonstrations, tomahawk throwing, and other demonstrations.

On the first Saturday in October, the locals get together to venerate their nearly two-century-old apple tree at the sensibly named **Old Apple Tree Festival** (360/619-1108, free). The festival focuses on environmental and historical preservation, and the Urban Forestry Commission is on hand to give away free cuttings from the legendary tree itself. In early October, don't miss the very popular **Fort Vancouver Candlelight Tours** with interpreters dressed in 1840s period clothing.

The **Christmas Ship Parade** (www.christmasships.org) is another favorite event, with decorated vessels plying the Columbia and Willamette Rivers on the second and third weeks of December. You'll also find Officers' Row decorated with traditional evergreens for the holidays, plus concerts and carriage rides to get you in the spirit of the holidays.

SHOPPING

The two-level **Vancouver Mall** (8700 NE Vancouver Mall Dr., 360/892-6255, www.westfield.com/vancouver) has over 115 shops, restaurants, and services, including JCPenney, Macy's, Nordstrom, Sears, and Old Navy. It is hard to miss at the junction of I-205 and Highway 500.

SPORTS AND RECREATION

The 14-foot-wide, paved **Columbia River Waterfront Trail** follows the shore eastward for 3.5 miles from downtown to Tidewater Cove. It's a wonderful place for a sunset stroll or bike ride. Find trailheads at Wintler Community Park, Marine Park, Waterfront Park or downtown Vancouver.

Vancouver Lake Park (6801 NW Lower River Rd., 360/487-7100, daily 7 A.M.–dusk, $3 cars, free for pedestrians and bikes), three miles west of downtown, is a local hot spot for both sailboarders and anglers. The nearly 300-acre strip of land offers picnicking, swimming, and fishing, plus grassy and shady areas. It is also home to one of the largest great blue heron rookeries in the region, and bald eagles can be found roosting in the trees during the winter months.

A 2.5-mile hiking trail connects Vancouver Lake park with **Frenchman's Bar Park** (9612 NW Lower River Rd., 360/619-1123, 7 A.M.–dusk daily, $3 cars, free for pedestrians and bikes) along the Columbia River, where there is a public beach for swimming, fishing access, and a very popular sand pit with eight volleyball courts set up in the summer.

There are no lifeguards at either park, which is why most families prefer **Salmon Creek Park** (off NW 117th St., 360/696-8171), a small lake with trained professionals on the lookout during the summer months.

ACCOMMODATIONS

While comfy lodging is plentiful on the Washington side of the river, dozens of motels and a hostel are also available in Portland, Oregon.

Under $100

Right in downtown Vancouver, near I-5, there is an **Econolodge** (601 Broadway, 360/693-3668, $70 s or $80 d) with standard motel rooms with fridges and microwaves. Whirlpool-bath rooms are also available.

For the touch of home that only a B&B can offer, try the **Briar Rose Inn** (314 W. 11th St., 360/694-5710, $75 d), a lovely 1908 Craftsman in the center of downtown. The four rooms, two of which have private baths, have wireless Internet, and the unbeatable "Grandma's house" feel of antique sumptuousness.

There are two Shilo Inn locations in the metropolitan Vancouver area. Pass up the one downtown on East 13th; it is ho-hum at best. Instead, visit **Shilo Inn & Suites Salmon Creek** (13206 NE Hwy. 99, 360/573-0511, www.shiloinns.com, $79–89 s or d) in Hazel Dell. It may not look special from the outside, but walk through the door and you'll see it is a class above most chains. The interiors are brand new and immaculate at this well-tended hotel. The property has a pool, spa, and sauna. Beds are comfortable and rooms have fridges and microwaves. There's also free Wi-Fi, continental breakfasts, and cookies during the day.

$100-150

Convenient to downtown and the fort district, **Red Lion Vancouver at the Quay** (100 Columbia St., 360/694-8341 or 800/733-5466, www.redlion.com, $100 s or $110 d) sits right at the base of the I-5 Interstate Bridge next to a 1.8-mile riverfront trail. Ask for a room with a view of the river to watch the lights of Portland twinkle over the Columbia. The furnishings and bathroom fixtures are a bit tired, but the rooms are clean and the linens are new. There's an outdoor pool, fitness center, business center, and a restaurant and lounge on premises. The hotel also offers free wireless Internet and a free Portland airport shuttle to its guests. Plus, it is pet-friendly.

East of downtown, just off of I-205, is **Phoenix Inn** (12712 SE 2nd Circle, 360/891-9777 or 888/988-8100, www.phoenixinnsuites.com, $129 s or $134 d) with 98 mini-suites. A free continental breakfast buffet is included, along with an indoor pool and hot tub.

$150-200

Residence Inn by Marriott (8005 NE Parkway Dr., Orchards, 360/253-4800 or 800/331-3131, www.residenceinn.com, $159 s or $189 d) has apartment-style rooms with kitchens and fireplaces, plus an outdoor pool, hot tub, and airport shuttle.

The **Heathman Lodge** (7801 NE Greenwood Dr., 360/254-3100 or 888/475-3100, www.heathmanlodge.com, $119–159 s or d) is not affiliated with the uber-luxurious Heathman Hotel across the Columbia in Portland, but it is one of the nicest hotels in Vancouver. It features spacious rooms and rustic lodge-style touches like wood beams, leather lampshades, and handcrafted furniture, as well as modern comforts like an indoor pool and complete exercise facility.

Homewood Suites by Hilton Hotel (701 SE Columbia Shores Blvd., 360/750-1100 or 800/225-5466, www.homewood-suites.com, $169 s or d) is a luxurious business hotel right on the Columbia River with kitchen suites.

$200-250

The Frank Lloyd Wright-esque **Bridge View Bed and Breakfast** (11734 SE Evergreen Hwy., 360/609-1381, www.bridgeviewbandb.com) was custom designed to pleasingly complement the aesthetics of the Glen Jackson Bridge under which it stands. The giant greatroom features a curving bank of floor-to-ceiling windows that presents views of this larger-than-life bridge and the Columbia River. The interior is also a compilation of luxe modern furnishings with shared amenities like a full kitchen, dining room, and living room with large-screen HDTV and surround sound. About 10 minutes east of downtown, the house has an upstairs master suite ($210) with a whirlpool tub, walk-in shower, and double-sink bathroom, plus a separate office with built-in cabinet desk. Downstairs are two standard rooms ($80) with double bed in each.

Camping

The closest public campgrounds are **Paradise Point State Park** (360/263-2350), 16 miles north on I-5 near Woodland, and **Battle Ground Lake State Park** (360/687-4621), 20 miles northeast of town in Battle Ground. Campsites are reservable May through September by calling 888/226-7688 or visiting www.parks.wa.gov.

Private parks in the area include **Vancouver RV Park** (7603 NE 13th Ave., 360/695-1158, $22–38) and **99 RV Park** (1913 NE Leichner Rd., 360/573-0351, $20–29) in Salmon Creek.

FOOD

It's a fact that many Vancouver locals cross the bridge into Portland for the bonanza of restaurants the big city offers. But for the smaller-town feel and the personal attention that comes with it, save the travel time and explore the local treats Vancouver has available.

Cafés

One place wins hands-down on the Vancouver breakfast front: **Dulin's Village Café** (1905 Main St., 360/737-9907, 7 A.M.–3 P.M. daily), with great home fries, omelettes, and whole-wheat pancakes. It's also popular at lunch with the downtown crowd.

Travelers can relax with an espresso and croissant at **Java House** (210 W. Evergreen Blvd., 6 A.M.–5 P.M. Mon.–Fri., 8 A.M.–2 P.M. Sat., closed Sun., 360/737-2925) or **Paradise Café** (1304 Main St., 360/696-1612, 7 A.M.–5 P.M. Mon.–Fri., 8 A.M.–4 P.M. Sat., closed Sun.). Paradise also has a deli with fresh sandwiches.

Tommy O's Aloha Café (210 W. Evergreen Blvd., 360/694-5107, 6 A.M.–9 P.M. Sun.–Thurs., 8 A.M.–9:30 P.M. Fri.–Sat.), at the Vancouver Market Place, has interesting and healthy lunches like stir-fry with tofu, teriyaki burgers, and spicy chicken or beef bento, as well as soups and sandwiches.

If you can handle the suited throngs that line up at **Rosemary Café** (1003 Main St., Vancouver, 360/737-7611) during workday lunch hour, your patience will be rewarded. This homey café in downtown Vancouver slaps together some of the best sandwiches the city has to offer. My fave is the super grilled cheese sandwich with multiple types of cheeses on parmesan artisan bread. Rosemary also mixes remarkably fresh salads and homemade soups—I haven't tried it, but I heard the lady next to me raving about the beer cheese soup.

Contemporary Northwest

Enjoy stylish lunches and dinners in an elegant, historic setting at **The Grant House** (1101 Officers' Row, 360/906-1101, www.restauranthr.com, entrées $22), which is right inside a historic officer's house in Vancouver's Historic Reserve. Pick from a menu of glazed, grilled, and baked seafood, chops, and chickens. The restaurant also throws open the doors on Sunday mornings to serve a special brunch menu.

Seafood

On the banks of the Columbia, **Joe's Crab Shack** (101 E. Columbia Way, 360/693-9211, 10 A.M.–10 P.M. Sun.–Thurs., 10 A.M.–11 P.M. Fri.–Sat.) makes up a mess of large and delectable portions of seafood.

Italian and Pizza

Try **Bortolami's Pizzeria** (9901 NE 7th Ave., 360/574-2598, www.bortolami.com, 11:30 A.M.–8 P.M. Mon.–Tues., 11:30 A.M.–9 P.M. Wed.–Thurs., 11:30 A.M.–10 P.M. Fri., noon–9 P.M. Sat., 1–8 P.M. Sun.) for gourmet pies and a good selections of microbrews on tap. Or mosey over to **Little Italy's Trattoria** (901 Washington St., 360/737-2363, http://littleitalystrattoria.com, 11 A.M.–9 P.M. Mon.–Thurs., 11 A.M.–10 P.M. Fri.–Sat., 1–9 P.M. Sun.), which not only has good pizzas, but also a satisfying selection of Italian pasta and lasagna.

There's nothing like a perfectly crafted plate of from-scratch pasta to bring out the flavors of a locally made merlot. **Café Al Dente Italian Restaurant and Wine Bar** (907 Main St., 360/696-3463, www.cafealdente.net, 11 A.M.–9 P.M. Tues.–Sat.) offers the ideal combination of delectable homemade pastas and sauces with winning wine pairings for a blissful culinary experience.

Thai

For an authentic taste of Asia, try **Thai Orchid Restaurant** (1004 Washington St., 360/695-7786, www.thaiorchidrestaurant.com, 11:30 A.M.–9:30 P.M. Mon.–Fri., noon–9:30 P.M. Sat.–Sun.), serving Thai curries, noodles, and desserts.

Greek

Hidden House is named for its builder, Lowell M. Hidden, and not for any difficulty you'll have finding it. **The Touch of Athens at Hidden House** (100 W. 13th St., 360/695-

6198, 11 A.M.–2 P.M. and 5–9 P.M. Mon.–Fri., 5–10 P.M. Sat.) offers traditional Greek foods and atmosphere, complete with belly dancing and accordion music on weekend evenings.

Pub Grub and Burgers

Hazel Dell Brew Pub (8513 NE Hwy. 99, 360/576-0996, www.hazeldellbrewpub.com, 11:30 A.M.–9 P.M. Mon., 11 A.M.–10 P.M. Tues.–Fri., noon–10 P.M. Sat., 4–9 P.M. Sun.) serves pub meals, including fish and chips, burgers, and pasta in a lively, noisy setting to accompany its 14 different brewed-on-the-premises beers. And the setting of **McMenamins of the Columbia Brew Pub** (1801 SE Columbia River Dr., 360/254-3950, www.mcmenamins.com, 11 A.M.–11 P.M. Sun.–Thurs., 11 A.M.–1 A.M. Fri.–Sat.) is sublime, sidled up to the river on Hidden Way just east of Marine Park.

The sporting set is always at home at **Out-A-Bounds** (14415 SE Mill Plain Blvd., 360/253-4789, 11 A.M.–1:30 A.M. daily), chowing down on traditional sports-bar fare like wings, burgers, and beer.

You'll find pretty much the best fast-food burgers in the state, if not all of the Pacific Northwest at **Burgerville USA** (www.burgerville.com)—yes, Seattleites, even better than Dick's. The flagship store (360/694-4971, 7 A.M.–10 P.M. daily) is at 7401 East Mill Plain Boulevard, where the first Burgerville opened in 1961 and let loose the goodness. But I find the coolest location is **Burgerville's second shop** (307 E. Mill Plain Blvd., 360/693-8801, 7 A.M.–10 P.M. Mon.–Sat., 8 A.M.–10 P.M. Sun.) ever opened; it's the only one that has been left as a walk-up stand, as it originally was built in the early 1960s. All of the food at any Burgerville is cooked with fresh ingredients, with a special focus on seasonal, local ingredients like thick-cut sweet Walla Walla onions for the fried rings and tart Northwest blackberries in the shakes and lemonade. The chain has a commitment to environmental sustainability and a policy of paying fair wages, so you're likely to be greeted with a smiling face when you step up to the counter.

Vancouver's best burgers are at Burgerville USA.

© ERICKA CHICKOWSKI

Markets

The **Vancouver Farmers Market** (5th and Ester Sts., 360/737-8298, http://vancouverfarmersmarket.com, 9 A.M.–3 P.M. Sat., 10 A.M.–3 P.M. Sun., Mar.–Oct.) takes place downtown. It's a great place to look for local produce, herbs, arts and crafts, baked goods, and entertainment.

INFORMATION AND SERVICES

For maps or other information, visit the **Washington State Visitor Information Center** (750 Anderson St., 360/750-1553, 8 A.M.–5 P.M. Mon.–Fri., 8:30 A.M.–5 P.M. Sat.–Sun.) located in the O. O. Howard House of Vancouver Historic Reserve. Also helpful is the **Greater Vancouver Chamber of Commerce** (404 E. 15th St., 360/694-2588 or 800/377-7084, www.vancouverusa.com), reachable by taking a left off the I-5 Mill Plain exit 1D.

The **Gifford Pinchot National Forest Supervisor's Office** (10600 NE 51st Circle, Orchards, 360/891-5000, 360/891-5009 for recorded recreation information, 8 A.M.–5 P.M. Mon.–Fri.) is in Vancouver. Stop by for details on Mount St. Helens and other nearby outdoor attractions.

Emergency medical services are provided by **Legacy Salmon Creek Hospital** at (2211 NE 139th St., 360/487-1000). Pet medical care is available at **VCA East Mill Plain Animal Hospital** (9705 East Mill Plain Blvd., 360/892-0032).

GETTING THERE AND AROUND

The local transit system is **C-TRAN** (360/695-0123, www.c-tran.com, $1.60–2.45 per ride, $3.85 all-day pass, $3.35 express ride to Portland), which provides daily service throughout Clark County, as well as to downtown Portland.

For cross-country trips, contact **Greyhound** (613 Main St., 360/696-0186 or 800/231-2222, www.greyhound.com).

Amtrak (360/694-7307 or 800/872-7245, www.amtrak.com) trains stop at a classic early-1900s depot at the foot of West 11th Street, with daily connections north and south on the Coast Starlight, and eastward up the Columbia River aboard the **Empire Builder.**

For air service, head south across the Columbia River to **Portland International Airport** (7000 NE Airport Way, Portland, OR, 877/739-4636, www.flypdx.com), second only in the Pacific Northwest to Sea-Tac International Airport. The airport is serviced by all the major domestic and international airline carriers and is a major hub for Alaska Airlines, which offer dozens of flights to Seattle, Spokane, and other nearby Northwest destinations.

The main parking lot is $24 per day or $3 per hour here, with long-term economy parking for $10 per day. Dozens of shuttle and van carriers service Vancouver from here, including **Blue Start Transportation Group** (800/247-2272, www.bluestarbus.com, $24–32), which offers door-to-door shuttle service.

Pearson Air Field (VUO, within Vancouver National Historic Reserve) provides services to private pilots.

Lewis and Clark Highway

While the trip along Highway 14, known also as Lewis and Clark Highway, does offer some beautiful Gorge scenery, by the time you arrive at Maryhill Museum you may feel that Columbia River trek is a bit longer than it looks on the map. This is truly a remote part of the state, so stock up on soft drinks, chips, and other necessities first.

Also keep your eyes peeled for speed limit signs. The now-you-see-'em, now-you-don't towns that you'll whiz by require slower speeds within their sometimes hard-to-gauge boundaries, creating speed traps that are zealously checked by local cops.

CAMAS AND WASHOUGAL AREA

While the sight and scent of the enormous Georgia-Pacific paper mill seem to dominate Camas, Camas and neighboring Washougal are attractive small towns right along the Columbia, with big trees lining the main route.

Sights and Recreation

The **Two Rivers Heritage Museum** (Front and 16th Streets, 360/835-8742, 11 A.M.–3 P.M. Tues.–Sat., $3 adults, $2 seniors, $1 ages 6–18) in Washougal has local historical artifacts and photos. A lovely walking path along the Columbia River levee leaves from Steamboat Landing Park in Washougal.

The **Rocket City Neon Museum** (1554 NE 3rd Ave., Camas, 360/571-5885) is one of the more unusual museums in Washington, with hundreds of neon signs, some more than 50 years old.

On Highway 14 between Washougal and North Bonneville, the **Cape Horn Viewpoint** (milepost 25) provides a good spot for photographing the dramatic west entrance to the Gorge and for viewing massive Beacon Rock.

For a short and scenic side trip, take Cape Horn Drive downhill to the river, through overhanging maples and Douglas fir trees.

Washougal's claim to fame is the **Pendleton Woolen Mill** (17th and A Sts., 503/226-4801 or 800/568-2480, www.pendleton-usa.com), in operation since 1912 and still producing its acclaimed woolen products. The mill gives guided tours by appointment. An outlet store here sells seconds and overstocked items.

Camas has a summer-only outdoor **swimming pool** (120 NE 17th, 360/834-2382).

Festivals and Events

Camas Days (360/834-2472), held annually on the fourth weekend of July, includes a parade, wine and microbrew street, live entertainment, craft and food booths, and of course, the bathtub races, which are not to be missed.

Accommodations and Food

For the most basic of accommodations, consider staying at the **Rama Inn** (544 6th St., Washougal, 360/835-8591, $55 s or $65 d), which has an outdoor pool on premises.

The stately colonial Greek-revival **Fairgate Inn** (2213 NW 23rd Ave, Camas, 360/834-0861, $125–175 d) makes an attractive alternative to more humble lodgings. All eight of the elegant rooms come complete with private bath, fireplace, high-speed Internet, and a full breakfast served in the dining room.

Information

Get answers to your questions at the **Camas-Washougal Chamber of Commerce** (422 NE 4th Ave., Camas, 360/834-2472, www .cwchamber.com, 9 A.M.–5 P.M. Mon.–Fri.).

◖ BEACON ROCK STATE PARK

Beacon Rock State Park (509/427-8265, www .parks.wa.gov) is 35 miles east of Vancouver on Highway 14, and just west of the little town of North Bonneville. You can't miss it; the centerpiece of the park is an 848-foot-high ancient volcano core believed to be the largest such

Climb to the top of Beacon Rock for amazing views of the Columbia River.

monolith in North America. Lewis and Clark named it when they traversed the Gorge in 1805.

Hike the steep one-mile trail to the pinnacle for spectacular views of the Gorge; the trail boasts a 15 percent grade, but handrails make the hiking both easier and safer. This and other trails provide 14 miles of hiking in the park. Advanced climbers only may attempt to climb on the south side of the rock, but it is closed part of the year to protect nesting hawks; register at the trailhead. The main part of the park is north of the highway, and old roads are perfect for mountain biking and horseback riding. A four-mile trail switchbacks to the 1,200-foot summit of **Hamilton Mountain**, passing the very scenic Rodney Falls. Anglers can launch their boats from the boat ramp to catch Columbia River white sturgeon, and campers can stay in the densely forested sites (no RV hookups) for $19, $10 for an extra vehicle. The campground is open April–October. A smaller state park campground below the noisy railroad tracks along the river is open all year, but there are no showers. Campers can take

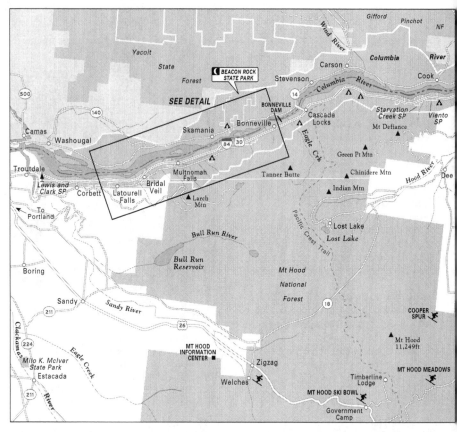

showers at the nearby private Beacon Rock RV Park (360/427-8473).

BONNEVILLE DAM AREA

Bonneville Dam snakes across the Columbia in three sections, connecting the shorelines and Bradford and Cascades Islands. This was the site of the famous Columbia River Cascades that made travel down the river so treacherous for Oregon Trail emigrants. An Army base, **Fort Cascades,** was constructed on the Washington side of the Cascades in the early 1850s and remained in use until 1861. Today, Fort Cascades Historic Site has an interesting 1.5-mile loop path with interpretive signs describing the area's rich history.

Bonneville Dam

The original Bonneville Dam and power plant were built here between 1933 and 1937; a second plant was added on the Washington shore in 1981. Together they produce over a million kilowatts of power that feed into the grid for the Northwest and California.

Visit the **Bonneville Second Powerhouse** visitors center (509/427-4281, 9 A.M.–5 P.M. daily, closed major holidays), on the Washington side of the Bonneville Dam, to see the inner workings of the powerhouse (including a peek inside a spinning turbine) and informative displays. You'll feel dwarfed by the enormity of the river, dam, and surrounding hills. Windows offer a chance to watch coho,

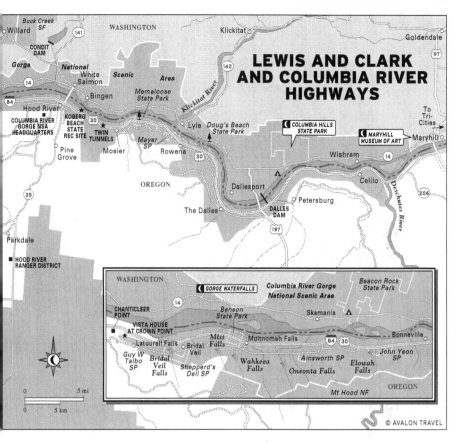

sockeye, and king salmon, along with steel-head, shad, lamprey, and other fish as they head upstream each summer and fall.

Cross **The Bridge of the Gods** ($1 toll for autos) into Oregon and visit the original **Bonneville Lock and Dam** (541/374-8820), a popular tourist spot with continuous presentations, exhibits, and fish viewing.

STEVENSON

The small town of Stevenson has been the governmental seat for Skamania County since 1893, but it is only now starting to come into its own. An enjoyable museum, one of the fanciest lodges in Washington, and hordes of summertime windsurfers and kiteboarders give life

to the awesome natural surroundings. **Rock Creek Park** (Rock Creek Dr. and Rock Creek Park Rd.) on the west side of town provides an excellent place for beginner sailboarders and kitesurfers to practice their art.

Columbia Gorge Interpretive Center

Located a mile west of Stevenson, this award-winning museum (990 SW Rock Creek Dr., 800/991-2338, www.columbiagorge.org, 10 A.M.–5 P.M. daily, closed Thanksgiving, Christmas, and New Year's Day, $7 adults, $6 seniors and students, $5 ages 6–12, free for kids under 6) looks across Rock Creek Cove to the mighty Columbia River. Highlights include an enormous simulated basalt cliff, with its crevices filled by Native American and pioneer artifacts, a 37-foot-high fish wheel, a restored Corliss steam engine, and Native American artifacts. Another section introduces you to the spiritual side of the Columbia Gorge. The museum also is home to objets d'art and furniture once belonging to Russian mystic Baron Eugene Fersen, along with the world's largest collection of rosaries. Special exhibits change frequently, and a museum store features the works of local artisans.

Wine Tours

Based in Stevenson, but running tours all along both sides of the scenic area, **Martin's Gorge Tours** (503/349-1323 or 877/290-8687, www.martinsgorgetours.com) specializes in running both small and large groups through the best of the area's wineries and waterfalls all year long, plus taking hikers on wildflower hunts during the colorful spring months. Run by a knowledgeable and affable guide, the service offers a laid-back way to check out big portions of the area while sipping vino without worry of driving impaired. The company's signature Wine and Waterfall Tour ($99) will take you on an all-day adventure through the Gorge that departs directly from several hotels on the stretch between Carson and Bingen.

Festivals and Events

The **Fourth of July** brings the usual fireworks, picnics, and concessions to Skamania County; the best way to see the fireworks is aboard the sternwheeler *Columbia Gorge* (503/224-3900, www.portlandspirit.com), which offers a special tour. In late July, the **Columbia Gorge Bluegrass Festival** (800/989-9178, www.columbiagorgebluegrass.net) brings foot-stompin' music, contests, dances, and plenty of food all day long at the Rock Creek Fairgrounds in Stevenson. The annual **Skamania County Fair and Timber Carnival** (509/427-3979), held in August, offers entertainment, a parade, timber contests, exhibits, and food. The fair prides itself on being one of the last original free fairs.

Sports and Recreation

Rent sailboards, kayaks, canoes, snowshoes, climbing gear, and mountain bikes from **Waterwalker** (21 Carson Depot Rd., 509/427-2727). This popular store also offers sailboard lessons most summer afternoons.

The **Skamania Lodge Golf Course** (SW Skamania Lodge Dr., 509/527-2541, www.skamania.com, $40–65) reigns as the nicest set of links the Gorge has to offer. With amazing Columbia cliff views, well-tended fairways and greens and a practice facility with a driving range, bunker, and chipping and putting greens, this is a true destination-style course.

Accommodations

The finest luxury resort in the Gorge, **Skamania Lodge** (1131 SW Skamania Lodge Dr., 509/427-7700 or 800/221-7117, www.skamania.com, $209–289 d) is a huge property sporting an indoor pool, sauna, hot tubs, fitness center, tennis courts, 18-hole golf course, hiking trails, and convention facilities. The lodge has a classic feeling. Its tall windows face the Columbia River and an enormous river rock fireplace heats up the lobby. Rooms come in various sizes and have views of the mountain or the river. Pet rooms are available for an additional fee. Inside is a small Forest Service **information center and bookshop** (509/427-2528, 9 A.M.–5 P.M. daily). It also hosts guest speakers each spring and fall.

If those rates are a little rich for your blood, **Columbia Gorge Riverside** (509/427-5650, www.cgriversidelodge.com, $79–199 d) offers a cozy atmosphere in its modern, well-appointed log cabins along the Columbia River near Stevenson. It has no phones or TVs, but each has a kitchen, back deck, and access to the hot tub.

Park RVs at **Lewis & Clark RV Park** (509/427-5982, $20 nightly) in North Bonneville, which offers well-spaced campsites on its grassy and tree-shaded property.

Food

Joe's El Rio (193 Hwy. 14, 509/427-4479, 4–9 P.M. daily) has authentic Mexican cuisine to eat in or carry out.

© ERICKA CHICKOWSKI

Skamania Lodge

Skamania Lodge serves gourmet Northwest cuisine three meals a day in an elaborate and busy setting. Be ready to drop $40 or more per person for dinner and be sure to get reservations, especially on summer weekends. The Sunday brunch is especially popular.

Information

The **Stevenson Chamber of Commerce and Visitor Information Center** (167 NW 2nd, 800/989-9178, www.skamania.org, 8 A.M.–5 P.M. daily in summer, Mon.–Fri. only in winter) is the place to go for the scoop on Stevenson.

Getting There

Bus service to these parts is close to nonexistent. Vancouver's **C-TRAN** (360/695-0123, www.c-tran.com) will get you as far east as Camas and Washougal. Cross over to the Oregon side for Greyhound bus service along I-84.

CARSON AREA

Just a few miles east of Stevenson is the little town of Carson, known for its hot springs and

as an entry point into Gifford Pinchot National Forest. The drive north from Carson to the east side of Mount St. Helens offers photographic and recreational opportunities aplenty.

Sights

Historic **Carson Hot Springs Resort** (509/427-8292 or 800/607-3678, www.carson hotspringresort.com) has been drawing visitors to its 126°F natural mineral baths since 1876. The St. Martin Hotel was built in 1897 and cabins were added in the 1920s. Hot mineral baths and wraps ($20), and one-hour massages ($60) are available and still the chief draw.

The **Big Lava Bed Geologic Area** encompasses 12,500 acres of lava beds, the eerie remains of an ancient volcano. The steep walls of the tree-covered crater rise 800 feet on the north end of the area, sheltering a meadow deep inside. When exploring the lava beds, be sure to bring plenty of water and keep track of your wanderings, since there are no marked trails to follow. It's even rumored to be haunted. Get here by heading north up Cook-Underwood Road from the town of Cook, eight miles east of Carson on Highway 14. It turns into South

Prairie Road (Forest Service Road 66) after several miles and continues to the lava beds, approximately 14 miles up. The road follows the east side of the lava for the next 10 miles or so.

Festivals and Events

For a walk far on the wild side, plan your trip to catch Carson's **Bigfoot Daze** festival, held on the last weekend of August every year. The wacky festival features talks and panels on the legendary beast plus a costume contest, Sasquatch yell contest, and a chili cook-off.

Sports and Recreation

Several day hikes await the adventurous, including the **Bob Kuse Memorial Trail,** leading to the 1,000-foot summit of **Wind Mountain,** a three-mile hike that provides dramatic views over the Columbia Gorge and a peek at historical Indian vision-quest sites. The trailhead is a mile up Wind Mountain Road on the east side. Be on the lookout for rattlesnakes during the summer months!

For a good view of the area's peaks, take a short hike to the top of **Little Huckleberry Mountain,** best hiked mid-July–October. Take Forest Service Road 66 (along the east edge of the lava bed) to the 49 trailhead; climb the steep grade for 2.5 miles to the summit and a refreshing berry break. The trail is open to hikers, equestrians, and mountain bikers.

A $5 National Forest Recreation Day Pass is required for parking at all Forest Service trailheads in the scenic area. Or pick up an annual **Northwest Forest Pass** ($30) that is valid for most national forest trailheads in Washington and Oregon. Get one from most local sporting-goods stores, any Forest Service office (800/270-7504), or at www.fs.fed.us/passespermits.

Accommodations and Food

Service is known to be a bit iffy, and even the recently renovated rooms are a bit creaky at **Carson Hot Springs Resort** (509/427-8292 or 800/607-3678, www.carsonhotspringresort .com). But the hotel rooms ($80 d) and basic cabins ($60 d) at this historic hot springs are a convenient stopover for those seeking a soak in the soothing spring water. Reserve early if you plan to stay on a weekend. The restaurant serves three meals a day, none of which is likely to wow you.

For something a little nicer, **【 Carson Ridge Cabins** (509/427-7777, $220–415) redefines "roughing it." The luxury cabins look out

© ERICKA CHICKOWSKI

Carson Ridge Cabins

to verdant Gorge and Cascade hillsides that can be enjoyed from each unit's private porch and charming log-swing. Rooms are decked out with all of the little amenities that add up to an epic vacation: whirlpool tubs controlled with wireless remotes, gas fireplaces,, plush robes, and big flat-panel televisions. Many of the wood furnishings are one-of-a-kind, custom-built pieces. Choose between enjoying the deliciously gourmet breakfast from a cozy dining area or have it directly delivered to your door for maximum privacy. If you can time it right, the property's monthly community dinner is a real treat.

Several Forest Service campgrounds are north of Carson off Wind River Road. Closest is **Panther Creek Campground** (open mid-May–mid-Nov.) nine miles up Wind River Road, and 1.5 miles up Forest Service Road 6517. This tranquil campground is on a stream and has water spigots and toilet facilities. **Beaver Campground** (mid-Apr.–Oct.) is 12 miles up Wind River Road and offers easy RV parking, fishing, and hiking. A shaded, lightly used respite, **Paradise Creek Campground** (mid-May–mid-Nov.) is 21 miles up Wind River Road, and another 6 miles on Forest Service Road 30. All three of these campgrounds range $17–34; make reservations ($9 extra) at 518/885-3639 or 877/444-6777.

Big Cedars County Park (north of Willard on Oklahoma Rd.) has 28 primitive campsites available; there are 23 more at **Home Valley County Park** (509/427-9478), along with a coin-operated shower. RVers can park at **Carson Hot Springs Resort** (509/427-8292).

WHITE SALMON AND BINGEN

Continuing eastward from Carson and Home Valley, the highway passes the trailhead (Forest Pass required for parking) for **Dog Mountain Trail,** a rugged, switchback-filled, 3.5-mile climb to the summit of this 2,900-foot peak. This is a good chance to stretch your legs and enjoy wildflower-filled meadows in spring. Beyond the trailhead, the Lewis and Clark Highway cuts through five short tunnels and the landscape begins to open up, with fewer trees and broader vistas. At Cook-Underwood Road, you'll encounter **Little White Salmon/Willard National Fish Hatchery** (13 miles east of Stevenson) and the **Spring Creek National Fish Hatchery** (2 miles west of the Hood River Bridge). Both are free to visit and open 7:30 A.M.–4 P.M. daily. Their goal is the reestablishment of a self-sustaining coho salmon fishery in the Wenatchee River Basin.

The German-themed speed-trap known as Bingen straddles Highway 14; its bigger twin, White Salmon, is just 1.5 miles up the hill. White Salmon has several Bavarian-style buildings and a 14-bell **glockenspiel** mounted above its city hall. The only one of its kind on the West Coast, it chimes hourly 8 A.M.–8 P.M. and plays music on holidays. East of these two towns, the road continues along the river's edge and through the tiny village of **Lyle.**

Gorge Heritage Museum

A well-preserved 1911 church provides the home of the **Gorge Heritage Museum** (202 E. Humbolt, Bingen, 509/493-3228, 11:30 A.M.–4:30 P.M. Thurs.–Sun. late May–Sept.). The collection includes local pioneer relics, Native American artifacts, and historic photos.

Wineries

Wineries around this stretch of Highway 14 fall within the Columbia River Gorge (www.columbiagorgewine.com) bi-state viticultural appellation. Standing as they are on the wetter side of the mountains, the vineyards here tend to produce more delicate wines than the rest of Central Washington. The region also makes for a change of scenery compared to the rest of Washington wine country, with vineyards surrounded by more trees and vegetation than wheat fields and sagebrush.

Set on a hill overlooking Mount Hood and the Gorge, **Wind River Cellars** (196 Spring Creek Rd., Husum, 509/493-2324, www.windrivercellars.com, 10 A.M.–6 P.M. daily, closed Dec. 15–Jan. 1, $5 tasting fee is waived if you purchase a bottle) is located off Highway 141 in Husum. Try the estate-grown white riesling in the tasting room, which is set within the winery's lovely cottage with sloping eaves and cedar deck.

Check out the all-natural winemaking process at **Klickitat Canyon Winery** (6 Lyle-Snowden Rd., Lyle, 509/365-2900, www.columbiagorgewinery.com), which prides itself on its from-the-earth methods. The wines here are fermented using only the yeast on the grapes—winemakers don't add any bi-sulfites and 100 percent of its grapes come from the Columbia Gorge, making its vintages a true reflection of the region's terroir. Klickitat offers tours and barrel room tastings noon–6 P.M. Saturday–Sunday.

Plan ahead and call **Gorge Crest Winery** (509/493-2026, www.gorgecrest.com) to schedule a tasting appointment in its modern but comfortable big red barn winery center. The grounds are gorgeous—a favorite for weddings.

Sports and Recreation
RIVER RAFTING
Between Klickitat Gorge and the White Salmon River, the area has enough thrills and spills for the hardest-core river rat. Here, you can find runs in the intermediate skill level class III up through the experts-only class V rapids, along with plenty of experienced pros to guide you through. The best rafting tends to run from May–June. Expect one-day trips to cost around $100, depending on your choice of runs.

Attracting some of the biggest names in the whitewater kayaking world, **Wet Planet** (860 Hwy. 141 in Husum, 877/390-9445, www.wetplanetwhitewater.com) offers a half-day trip through the Wild and Scenic White Salmon River that ends in a rollercoaster ride down the 13-foot Husum Falls. This outfitter takes you through some of the prettiest and most exciting portions of the upper White Salmon from a private put-in that's 2.1 miles upstream from where most local outfitters launch. If you're feeling particularly adventurous, try leaping off a basalt ledge into the river on the trip's optional cliff jump.

All Rivers Adventures (800/743-5628, www.alladventuresrafting.com) provides full-service river guidance and even owns a private ranch available for barbecues and volleyball

canoeing the White Salmon River

© ERICKA CHICKOWSKI

after your run. **Blue Sky Outfitters** (800/228-7238, www.blueskyoutfitters.com) guides one-day and overnight trips. **Wildwater River Tours** (800/522-9453, www.wildwater-river.com) takes a wide variety of trips and even offers guide training, if white water truly gets in your blood.

HORSEBACK RIDING
North Western Lake Riding Stables (509/493-4965, www.nwstables.com) has horseback rides near White Salmon ranging $40–160 per person. Rides can be had between 8 A.M. and sunset, weather permitting.

BIKE RENTALS
Cross the river to Oregon to pick up a rental bike at **Discovery Bikes** (116 Oak St., Hood River, Oregon, 541/386-4820, $20–55 per day), which keeps a huge corral of mountain bikes, road bikes, and kiddie bikes with training wheels on hand for visitors.

Festivals and Events
White Salmon's **Spring Festival** (509/365-4565, www.whitesalmonspringfestival.com) on the third weekend of May in Rheingarten Park includes a parade, food, entertainment, and a chili cook-off. Or, for some autumnal fun, pay a visit to Bingen's **Huckleberry Fest** (509/637-0411, www.huckleberryfest.com) on the second weekend of September. The parade and talent show play second fiddle to the main attraction: the huckleberry products. If it can be made with huckleberries, you can try it here.

Accommodations
A cozy inn with a long history is **Inn of the White Salmon** (172 W Jewett Blvd., 509/493-2335 or 800/972-5226, www.innofthe whitesalmon.com, $90 s or $106–135 d) in White Salmon. This homey hideaway features charming decor, wireless Internet, a fireplace, hot tub, and delicious gourmet breakfasts. Most rooms have private baths, but if you're looking for a bargain, ask about the eight-bed hostel room ($25 per person).

For a break from the norm, the **Columbia**

River Gorge Hostel (Humboldt and Cedar Streets, 509/493-3363, www.bingenschool.com) might be just your style. This restored 1938 schoolhouse offers 48 hostel beds ($19 pp) and six private rooms ($49 d). This place is a big hit with visiting windsurfers and rock climbers—so much so that windsurfing rentals and lessons are offered on-site and one of the Inn's amenities is a private climbing wall. A weight room, indoor basketball court, and kitchen area are among the hostel amenities. The Inn is home to memorabilia from the old school days. Reservations are recommended in midsummer.

Right on the northern side of the Hood River Bridge, **Bridge RV Park and Campground** ($39) runs a well-manicured park with riverfront access and pretty views of the Gorge. Its location puts it within easy striking distance of Hood River and all of the Washington-side recreation activities. With full hookups for RV campers and shady tent spots, plus a spic-and-span shower and laundry facilities, this is a comfortable camping spot to serve as base camp for multiday Gorge explorations.

Food
Those craving a hearty breakfast can count on satisfaction at **Big River Diner** (740 E. Steuben St., Bingen, 509/493-1414, 8 A.M.–8 P.M. daily), which serves ample portions of old favorites like biscuits and gravy, pancakes, and eggs.

For something homier, **Inn of the White Salmon** (509/493-2335) pulls out its dining chairs to nonguests who'd like to partake in its locally famous country breakfasts ($10). Phone ahead for reservations.

The wine and brewery scene has definitely benefited White Salmon from a culinary perspective, as the area is slowly attracting chefs interested in the region's legacy in vino and fresh produce. **Henni's Kitchen and Bar** (120 E Jewett, 509/493-1555, 5–9 P.M. daily) is a testament to that. A gastropub-style establishment with exposed brick walls and moody lighting, the wine and beer selection is extensive and daring and the bartenders also know how to make a mean cocktail to go along with the selection of small plates and gourmet entrées like pork loin stuffed with apricot sausage over polenta and green beans or house-made gnocci with chanterelle mushrooms and spinach in leek cream.

Road-trippin' families toting little ones should consider unloading the minivan at **Solstice Wood Fire Café** (415 W. Steuben St., Bingen, 509/493-4006, www.solsticewood firecafe.com, 11:30 A.M.–2 P.M. and 5–8 P.M. Mon.–Thurs., 11:30 A.M.–2 P.M. and 5–9 P.M. Fri., 11:30 A.M.–9 P.M. Sat., 11:30 A.M.–8 P.M. Sun.). This kid-friendly restaurant has a special play area and a chalkboard for the kids to unload a little of that pent-up road trip energy. The food's delish, too, with a menu full of wood-fired pizzas, sandwiches, and salads. The pizzas range from plain for picky eaters to inventive, such as the combo with chicken, potatoes, and sweet peppers.

Information and Services

Get regional information from the **Mount Adams Chamber of Commerce** (509/493-3630, business.gorge.net/mtadamschamber, 8 A.M.–5 P.M. daily June–Sept., Mon.–Fri. only the rest of the year) next to the toll bridge just west of Bingen.

Emergency medical services are provided by **Skyline Hospital** (211 Skyline Dr., 509/493-1101) in White Salmon. Pets can go to **Alpine Veterinary Hospital** (208 Lincoln Dr., 509/493-3908) in Bingen.

Getting There

The Bingen **Amtrak** (509/248-1146 or 800/872-7245, www.amtrak.com) station is located at 800 Northwest 6th Street. Service is daily, heading west to Vancouver and Portland, and east to Wishram, Pasco, Spokane, and all the way to Chicago.

LYLE TO WISHRAM

A transformation begins east of the Lyle area as the country opens up into rolling dry hills of grass and rock. In this desolate place the rumble of long freight trains and the sounds of tugs pushing barges upriver mingle with those of nature to create a hauntingly resounding symphony.

Wineries

There are no gimmicky attractions or kitschy gift shops at **Syncline Wine Cellars** (111 Balch Rd., 509/365-4361, www.syncline wine.com). Nope, it's all about the wine here at this family-run vintner that's tucked away on a piece of country property up in the hills above Lyle. The tasting room is simply a marble-topped bar placed in the corner of the property's barrel room, giving the vino center stage. Known best for its work with rhone and burgundy varietals, this winery's prized vintage is its cuvee elena, a blend of grenache, mourvedre, syrah and carignan.

A super-fun winery located on a remote stretch of road near Columbia Hills State Park, **Marshal's Winery** (158 Oak Creek Dr., 509/767-4633) never takes itself too seriously. The tasting room is done up similar to your grandad's rumpus room, with picnic tables adorned with simple tablecloths and serving M&Ms and Cheetos as palate cleansers. Marshall's bold barbera is the highlight here.

© ERICKA CHICKOWSKI

Marshal's Winery

© ERICKA CHICKOWSKI

petroglyphs at Columbia Hills State Park

◖ Columbia Hills State Park

With dramatic views of the river, an amazing collection of some of the oldest petroglyphs and pictographs in the Northwest and plenty of opportunity for recreation, Columbia Hills State Park stands out as one of the jewels of the Gorge's hot and grassy dry side. Located two miles east of Highway 197 on Highway 14, the park has good trout and bass fishing at Horsethief Lake, accessible from your boat or one of the park's rentals, with two boat launches—one on the lake, one on the river. Nearby is 500-foot-high **Horsethief Butte,** a favorite of rock climbers. And finally, the park's most draw-worthy asset is its collection of petroglyphs and pictographs, which were transplanted here after being carved off the nearby cliffsides to make way for The Dalles Dam. The campground at the park (509/767-1159, open Apr.–Oct.) has four standard sites ($17), eight partial utility sites ($23), six primitive sites ($12), a dump station, and a restroom.

Doug's Beach State Park

This tiny park is a staging area for the throngs of windsurfers who come here all summer long to play on the Columbia River. This is not a place for beginners since the swells can reach six–eight feet at times. There's no water or camping, but it does have outhouses. The park is located 2.5 miles east of the town of Lyle along Highway 14, and 7 miles west of Columbia Hills State Park. Park hours are 6:30 A.M.–dusk in summer and 8 A.M.–dusk in winter.

Getting There

Amtrak (800/872-7245, www.amtrak.com) trains stop at the little settlement of Wishram, nine miles east of The Dalles dam. Service is daily, heading west to Bingen, Vancouver, and Portland, and east to Pasco, Spokane, and continuing all the way to Chicago.

GOLDENDALE AREA

Highway 97 heads north from the Columbia to the little town of Goldendale, 10 miles away, passing scores of cows, happily munching away or taking it easy along the route. The horizon is dominated by the snowcapped summits of Mount Hood to the south and Mount Adams, Mount St. Helens, and Mount Rainier to the west. North of Goldendale, Highway 97 climbs through ponderosa pine forests as it reaches 3,107-foot **Satus Pass,** before descending into the scenic and lonely Yakama Reservation, and finally the town of Toppenish in Yakima Valley, 50 miles away. Goldendale began when the first farmers and loggers settled here in 1879 and has grown slowly over the decades since.

Sights and Recreation

Goldendale's 20-room **Presby Mansion** (127 W. Broadway, 509/773-4303, 10 A.M.–4 P.M. Mon.–Thurs., 9 A.M.–5 P.M. Fri.–Sun. mid-Apr.–mid-Oct., $4.50 adults, $1 ages 6–12, free for children under age 6) is the home of **Klickitat County Historical Museum.** Built in 1902, this magnificent white-clapboard mansion is filled with pioneer furnishings,

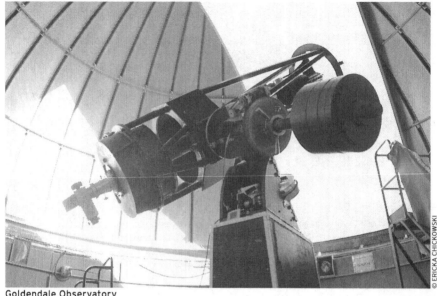

© ERICKA CHICKOWSKI

Goldendale Observatory

historic photos, farm equipment, and other artifacts. Be sure to check out the annual Christmas lighting party on the first Sunday of December.

Head a mile north of town and up-hill through open ponderosa pine forests to **Goldendale Observatory State Park** (509/773-3141, www.parks.wa.gov), where you'll find one of the nation's largest tele-scopes open to public viewing as well as sev-eral smaller portable telescopes. Take a tour and enjoy free audiovisual programs, displays, and demonstrations 2–5 P.M. and 8–mid-night Wednesday–Sunday April–September, 2–5 P.M. and 7–10 P.M. Friday–Sunday in winter.

Festivals and Events
G'day Goldendale Community Days (509/773-3677) in early July features arts and crafts, ethnic food, a flea market, antique auc-tion, beer garden, and parade. If the antique auction doesn't get your adrenaline pump-ing quite enough, check out Goldendale's

annual **4th of July Demolition Derby and Motocross Race** (509/250-0206) at the Klickitat County Fairgrounds. The **Klickitat County Fair and Rodeo** (509/773-3900) is an-other thrill-ride held over Labor Day weekend, including a carnival, parade, and chute after chute of angry bulls! This is one little town that knows how to do "extreme."

Accommodations
Lodging options are few and far between in this area. The best choice in town is **Quality Inn** (808 E. Simcoe Dr., 509/773-5881 or 800/358-5881, $89 s or $99 d), which sports a seasonal outdoor pool, continental breakfast, and clean motel units. The price is a little over the top, mostly because they know they've gotcha.

A cheaper alternative is the **Ponderosa Motel** (775 E. Broadway St., 509/773-5842, $60 s or $70 d), which is not quite as nice as the Quality Inn, but makes up for it with friendly and attentive service.

Out in the pine country north of Goldendale, **Pine Springs Resort** (2471 Hwy.

97, 509/773-4434, www.pinespringsresort
.net) is a neighborly retreat offering small cabins ($89), RV hookups ($22) and tent camping ($13). The social center of the place is a cozy snack bar with a rustic pine counter and stools and a big-screen TV. Also on premises are a game room, laundry room, grocery store, and gift shop. Dogs are welcome, and rates include free wireless Internet access.

Camp at **Brooks Memorial State Park** (509/773-4611, www.parks.wa.gov), 15 miles north of Goldendale on Highway 97. Tent ($19) and full-utility RV ($27) sites on 700 forested acres are available year-round. Enjoy the nine miles of hiking trails through cool coniferous forests and good trout fishing in the Klickitat River. The park has great cross-country skiing in winter, too.

Food

Tucked away into a restored Folk Victorian cottage on a quiet downtown Goldendale street, **The Glass Onion** (604 S. Columbus Ave., 509/773-4928, www.theglassonionrestau rant.com, 11 A.M.–4 P.M. Wed., 11 A.M.–9 P.M. Thurs.–Sat.) is a secret little treasure that foodies will want to take a detour to visit while rambling the vineyards of the Gorge. The seasonal menu is short, but every dish is an artfully plated symphony of flavors, such as the from-scratch pea soup and the grilled pork tenderloin served with ratatouille. Don't skip a salad with that entrée—they are as fresh as it gets. Check out the fine-art photos displayed on the walls while waiting for your dishes— they're taken by the chef's wife, a professional photographer.

For more day-to-day fare, **Gee's Family Restaurant** (118 E Main St., Goldendale, 509/773-6999, 10:30 A.M.–9:30 P.M. Mon.–Sat., 11:30 A.M.–8:30 P.M. Sun.) has decent Americanized Chinese dishes. Interestingly enough, it also grills up Goldendale's best burgers. These suckers are big enough for a couple of lumberjacks to split.

Sodbuster's Restaurant (1040 E. Broadway, Goldendale, 509/773-6160, 6 A.M.–9 P.M. Mon.–Sat., 6 A.M.–8 P.M. Sun.)

is also a reliable choice with its versatile diner menu. It's got the best breakfast fare in town.

Information and Services

For local information, stop by **Goldendale Chamber of Commerce** (903 E. Broadway, 509/773-3400, www.goldendalechamber.org, 9 A.M.–3 P.M. daily June–Sept., Mon.–Fri. only the rest of the year).

Emergency medical services are provided by **Klickitat Valley Hospital** (310 S. Roosevelt, 509/773-4022), while ailing pets can find succor at **Mid-Columbia Veterinary Clinic** (417 E. Broadway, 509/773-4363).

MARYHILL

Named after the daughter of businessman Sam Hill, the little settlement of Maryhill now boasts just 38 permanent residents. Hill dreamed that his town would one day become a thriving Quaker settlement, a wish that never materialized. The railroad man and campaigner for good roads left his mark nevertheless.

Although many of his original town buildings burned, Hill's mansion and the scale replica he built of Stonehenge as a war memorial still stand as a symbol of his hopes. The dusty intersection of Highways 14 and 97 may be remote, but it offers the wandering traveler some unique sights and some wonderful wines to add to the mystique of this place.

Sights

◖ MARYHILL MUSEUM OF ART

You'd be hard-pressed to find a collection more wonderfully eclectic than that of the Maryhill Museum of Art (35 Maryhill Museum Dr., 509/773-3733, www.maryhillmuseum.org, 9 A.M.–5 P.M. daily Mar. 15–Nov. 15, closed the rest of the year, $7 adults, $6 seniors, $2 ages 6–16, free for kids under 6). The beautiful 1914 concrete-and-steel home was originally built as a mansion for Sam Hill but now houses exhibits ranging from an extensive selection of Auguste Rodin sculpture to hundreds of international chess sets to a full gallery of memorabilia related to Queen Marie of Romania, a close friend of Sam Hill's. Along

CASTLE NOWHERE

The Northwest has no Hearst Castles or Winchester Mystery Houses, no Death Valley Scotties. In that favorite tourist category of eccentric mansions, the Northwest offers only the **Maryhill Museum of Art,** a place whose evolution from barren hillside to empty palatial home to museum took 26 years.

The museum – jokingly called "Castle Nowhere" – stands in isolated splendor on a bleak, sagebrush-strewn section of desert along the Columbia River, 100 miles east of Portland and Vancouver and 60 miles south of Yakima. This was just the setting that Seattle attorney and entrepreneur Sam Hill wanted when he was searching for a home site early in the 20th century.

Hill's most extravagant venture was an attempt to establish a utopian Quaker town "where the rain of the west and the sunshine of the east meet." He purchased 7,000 acres on the north side of the Columbia River south of Goldendale, and in 1914 began building his concrete palace, which was to be the farm's centerpiece. He named the spread Maryhill, after his wife, daughter, and mother-in-law, all three named Mary Hill. Hill attempted to interest Quakers in investing in his community. He built them a meeting hall and a few other facilities as enticement, but the Quakers declined. His wife, too, refused to live in this godforsaken place, taking the children and returning to Minnesota. All of the buildings constructed for the utopian town were destroyed in a fire in 1958.

About three miles upriver from the museum, just east of Highway 97, Hill built a concrete **replica of England's Stonehenge,** as it might have looked when intact, and dedicated it to the Klickitat County soldiers who died in World War I. Hill also built the **Peace Arch** that marks the U.S./Canadian border at Blaine, Washington.

The World War I years saw the mansion incomplete and bereft of inhabitants. After the war, President Herbert Hoover appointed Hill to a commission to help with Europe's reconstruction. There he met the three women who were responsible for Maryhill becoming a museum: Loie Fuller, a modern-dance pioneer at the Folies Bergère; Alma Spreckels, of a prominent California sugar family; and Queen Marie of Romania, whose country Hill aided during the post-war recovery period.

Fuller was particularly enthusiastic about the project and introduced Hill to members of the Parisian artistic community. Hill soon bought a large Auguste Rodin collection of sculptures and drawings.

When the 1926 dedication of the still-unfinished museum neared, Queen Marie agreed to come to New York and cross America by train to attend the ceremonies. She brought along a large collection of furniture, jewelry, clothing, and religious objects to be donated to the museum. Today her collection is one of the museum's largest.

Hill died in 1931 and was interred just below

with the surprisingly large permanent collection, Maryhill attracts top-notch traveling exhibits as well. Be sure to enjoy a moment on the patio watching the peacocks roam the grounds while enjoying the Columbia River vistas that brought Sam Hill here.

WINERIES
Overlooking the depths of the Gorge, **Cascade Cliffs Winery** (8866 Hwy. 14, 509/767-1100, www.cascadecliffs.com, 10 A.M.–6 P.M. daily) produces some deliciously obscure red wines.

The winery has the distinction of bringing the first Washington-grown barbera wine to market and is one of the few Washington wineries to produce nebbiolo. The exposed-beam warehouse tasting room (11 A.M.–5 P.M. Fri.–Sun. Apr.–Nov.) gives visitors the opportunity to sample wines.

The real centerpiece of the Gorge's winery scene, **Maryhill Winery** (9774 Highway 14, Goldendale, 877/627-9445, www.maryhill winery.com, 10 A.M.–6 P.M. daily) sits next door to the museum on a terraced cliff over

LEWIS AND CLARK HIGHWAY

the Stonehenge monument, overlooking the river. At the time of Hill's death, the museum still wasn't quite complete. Alma Spreckels took over the project, donating many pieces from her extensive art collection and seeing to it that the museum was finished and opened in 1940. On that occasion *Time* magazine called it "the loneliest museum in the world."

Sam Hill's original 7,000-acre spread remains intact, and the museum of sculpture, art, and trappings of Romanian and Russian nobility is worth the drive into the hinterlands. Standing on the veranda might feel a bit lonely, but the view is breathtaking and helps answer the question, "What in Sam Hill was he thinking?"

© ERICKA CHICKOWSKI

Stonehenge replica at Maryhill

Maryhill State Park's lush vegetation. Its comfortable tasting room and patio afford the most breathtaking scenery at any winery in the state. Much of the vineyard sits on a level below the tasting room terrace, its rows seemingly extending to the very lip of the Gorge. The panoramic view of the vineyard, the Gorge, and Mount Hood in the background make for unbelievable sunsets. The patio is pleasant when the wind doesn't whip up too much, and the tasting room itself is an elegant affair with a river-rock fireplace and an enormous 12-foot-

high oak and inlaid mirror bar built during the turn of the 20th century. Also on the premises right next to the winery arbor and tasting room is the brand new 4,000-seat Maryhill Winery Amphitheater, which draws summertime shows such as B. B. King and Crosby, Stills and Nash.

STONEHENGE REPLICA

Three miles east of Maryhill is another unexpected attraction. On a hilltop surrounded by open grass and sage sits a poured-concrete **replica of England's Stonehenge** (7 A.M.–10 P.M. daily) but with all the monoliths neatly aligned. Built by Sam Hill, an ardent Quaker and pacifist, the array is a monument to Klickitat county's 13 men who lost their lives in World War I. It is meant to illustrate the needless human sacrifice of war and is believed to be the nation's first World War I memorial. The ashes of Sam Hill himself are in an urn just down the slope from Stonehenge.

ORCHARDS AND FRUIT STANDS

Just down the hill from the Stonehenge replica are fruit orchards surrounding the small settlement of Maryhill, with its New England–style white church and old steam engine. The **Maryhill Fruit Stand** and **Gunkel Orchards** sell some of the finest peaches, apricots, cherries, and other fresh fruits that you'll ever taste.

Sports and Recreation

Maryhill State Park (509/773-5007) is five miles east of the Maryhill Museum and right along the Columbia River near the intersection of Highways 14 and 97. Maryhill State Park offers Columbia River waterfront access for boating, windsurfing, and fishing. A $7 fee grants you all-day access to one of two boat launches and a nearby dock. Once you dry off, you can also unwind taking a stroll and looking for waterfowl along 1.1 miles of trails here. The park is open for day use 6:30 A.M.–dusk in summer and 8 A.M.–dusk the rest of the year. You can also camp here year-round, in 50 full-utility RV campsites ($24), 20 standard tent sites ($17), and showers. Make reservations ($7 extra) at 888/226-7688 or www .parks.wa.gov. A **Travel Information Center** here has Columbia Gorge and Washington State information seasonally.

You can also camp or park RVs along the river at **Peach Beach Campark** (509/773-4698).

EAST TO TRI-CITIES

The stretch of Highway 14 between Maryhill and McNary Dam is some of the most sparsely populated country in Washington. Dry grassy hills provide grazing land for cattle, and a few scattered old farmsteads are slowly returning to the land. The land is bisected by tall power lines marching like misshapen insects over the landscape. There's not much traffic here, so tune in to the Spanish-language radio station, KDNA (FM 91.9) for music. Two bucolic settlements—**Roosevelt** and **Paterson**—are the only signs of human life on this side of the Columbia.

John Day Lock and Dam

The John Day Lock and Dam, 24 miles upriver from The Dalles and 6 miles east of Stonehenge, gave birth to Lake Umatilla and produces enough electricity for two cities the size of Seattle. Here you'll find one of the largest single-lift locks in the world, hefting vessels 113 feet. At the dam on Oregon's I-84, enjoy the fish-viewing room, visitors' gallery, and Giles French Park, which has a boat launch, a picnic area, and fishing.

A good portion of the power generated is used in the enormous Columbia Aluminum Corporation plant that stretches for two-thirds of a mile next to the dam. Camp for free at undeveloped **Cliffs Park,** approximately three miles off the highway on John Day Road.

Bickleton

For a pleasant side trip, drive north from Roosevelt to the farming town of Bickleton, with a friendly café on one side of the street and a tavern on the other. Bickleton has the unique distinction of being the bluebird capital of the world; houses for the little guys are everywhere. The bluebird housing project started in the 1960s when Jess and Elva Brinkerhoff built one, then another and another, and soon it was a community project. When the birds leave for the winter, the 700 houses are taken down, cleaned, and painted if they need it. Spring is the best time to view the bluebirds, but you're likely to see them all summer long.

In Cleveland Pioneer Park, four miles west of town, is a delightful old **carousel** with 24 wooden horses and a musical calliope. Built at the turn of the 20th century, the carousel has been here since 1928 and is a rare type that moves around a track. The horses are locked away in a secret location with the exception of a two-day period each summer: during the **Alder Creek Pioneer Picnic and Rodeo** in mid-June. This is the oldest rodeo in the state of Washington and also a cheap thrill at only $7.

For another piece of history, visit **Bluebird Inn** (121 E. Market St., 509/896-2273), said to be Washington's oldest tavern. Built in 1892, it has a classic century-old Brunswick pool table with leather pockets (still in use), along with other local artifacts.

The **Whoop-N-Holler Ranch Museum** (East Rd. between Bickleton and Roosevelt, 509/896-2344, 10 A.M.–4 P.M. Apr.–Sept., $3) contains a lifetime of collecting by Lawrence and Ada Whitmore. Two large buildings are filled with antique cars, as well as local historical items and family heirlooms that tell the interesting story of the Whitmore family. This is one of the largest collections of antique and classic cars in the state.

Wineries

Get lost in the sweet desolation of the Horse Heaven Hills viticultural region. Call ahead and make an appointment with **Destiny Ridge Vineyard** (509/786-3497), estate vineyard of Prosser-based Alexandria Nicole Cellars and a major grower for dozens of other wineries. Take in the sweeping views of the Columbia River as winemakers take you on a 2.5-hour tour ($35) of the vineyards followed by a barrel room tasting with light hors d'oeuvres. The vineyard also recently began a "glam-camp" program. Cozy up in a 14- by 17-foot platform tent equipped with electricity and water. Campers will be serviced with food to fire up a barbecue dinner and a breakfast in the vineyards for a one-of-a-kind getaway. Call for pricing.

Also here in the hills of the state's most remote region, **Columbia Crest Winery** (Hwy. 221, Columbia Crest Dr., Paterson, 509/875-2061, www.columbia-crest.com, 10 A.M.–4:30 P.M. daily) is perched just north of Paterson with its own commanding view across

the Columbia River and adjacent vineyards. Founded in 1962, and now one of Washington's largest wine producers, Columbia Crest operates much of the winery below ground, making it easier to maintain cool temperatures throughout the year.

Crow Butte State Park

Located at the site of one of many camps used by the Lewis and Clark Expedition, this 1,312-acre park sits along a lonesome stretch of highway halfway between the little towns of Roosevelt and Paterson. It offers boating, swimming, fishing, and waterskiing, with tent ($19) and RV sites ($24) and coin-operated showers. The campground is open daily late March–late October, plus winter weekends. Make reservations ($7 extra) at 888/226-7688 or www.parks .wa.gov. Crow Butte State Park covers half of an island created when the John Day Dam backed up the river to form Lake Umatilla; the other half is within **Umatilla National Wildlife Refuge** (509/546-8300, http://midcolumbiariver.fws.gov/Umatillapage.htm), which straddles both sides of the Columbia. A 0.75-mile trail leads to the top of Crow Butte (671 feet), with views across the Columbia to Mount Hood when the weather permits; keep your eyes open for rattlesnakes. The Umatilla National Wildlife Refuge has an overlook a few miles east of Crow Butte where you can peer across the river below while browsing a brochure describing the refuge and its abundant waterfowl.

McNary Dam

By the time you reach the McNary Dam area, the land has opened into an brushy desert of sage and grass broken only by center-pivot irrigation systems. The Columbia River's McNary Lock and Dam, 30 miles south of Pasco in Umatilla, Oregon, creates 61-mile-long Lake Wallula, which reaches up past the Tri-Cities to Ice Harbor Dam.

The **McNary National Wildlife Refuge,** next to McNary Dam, has a mile-long hiking trail popular with bird-watchers. Area species include hawks, golden and bald eagles, and prairie falcons.

Information and Services

This is remote country; the combined population of Roosevelt and Paterson is a minuscule 301. As a result, services are extremely limited. If you're coming from the west and your gas tank isn't full, be sure to take the 30-minute side trip up to Goldendale to fill up. From the west or north, gas up in the Tri-Cities or Prosser. Failing to do so could wreck a trip, leaving you stranded for hours in the hot sun.

If you're starving, Roosevelt has a very basic roadhouse establishment, **M&T Bar & Grill** (215 Roosevelt Ave., Roosevelt, 509/384-9440). Paterson has no restaurant, but it does have the small **Paterson Store** (48201 Paterson Ave., 509/875-2741) with basic provisions.

Columbia River Highway

The Oregon side of the Columbia River offers the fastest routes east to the warmer part of the region via I-84, which runs the length of the Gorge and then some. But there are also plenty of opportunities along this route to take it slow along impressive historic back roads and enjoy the sprays and cascades of one of the prettiest collections of waterfalls in the lower 48.

TROUTDALE

Known as the Gateway to the Gorge, Troutdale is the first town you'll encounter when getting off I-84 to take the slower, more scenic Historic Columbia River Highway through some of the best parts of the southern Gorge. It makes for a good stop to gather last-minute details about scenic points along the way and fill up gas tanks and bellies on the way in or out.

Sights

If you can get the timing down just right, the Troutdale Historical Society (503/661-2164, www.troutdalehistory.org) runs an inviting trio of museums that it opens up on the third Saturday of each month between 10 A.M. and 2 P.M. or by appointment. Built in 1900 by the son of Troutdale's founder, the **Harlow House Museum** (726 E. Historic Columbia River Hwy.) features period furnishings and several collections from local families that include vintage hats and ruby glass. The **Barn Museum** (726 E. Historic Columbia River Hwy.) features a growing collection of old farm equipment and other rotating exhibits. And the **Rail Depot Museum** (473 E. Historic Columbia River Hwy.) displays over 100 years' worth of train memorabilia, along with a Union Pacific caboose outside. In addition to the Saturday hours, this museum is also open 10 A.M.–4 P.M. Tuesday through Friday. It's located right at Depot Park, a pretty little municipal green space with access to the Sandy River and Beaver Creek.

Entertainment and Events

No need to dust off the ol' tuxedo to order a cocktail at **Shaken Martini Lounge** (101 W Historic Columbia River Hwy., 503/512-7485), but be ready to drink it up Bond-style at this 007-inspired lounge. The drinks are named after various Bond girls, decor is done up in sleek reds and blacks, and on Thursday nights the owner even shows Bond movies. If that sounds a might fancy for your tastes, head down the street to **Brass Rail Tavern** (108 E Historic Columbia River Hwy., 503/666-8756), a good old fashioned hole-in-the-wall that'll do right by you with a pool table, plenty of pitchers to pour and a game on the TV.

The many pubs of **McMenamins Edgefield Resort** (2126 SW Halsey St., 503/669-8610, www.mcmenamins.com) are like an amusement park for drinkers. Click together the billiard balls at Lucky Staehly's Pool Hall, pay homage to the Grateful dead at the tiny Jerry's Ice House, and check out the pipe sculptures and woodstove at the Distillery Bar, all of which are just a few of the drinking establishments set on the unique property.

Shopping

Troutdale is also the gateway to shopping deals as the home to the **Columbia Gorge Premium Outlets** (450 NW 257 Way, 503/669-8060, wwww.premiumoutlets.com/columbiagorge, 10 A.M.–8 P.M. Mon.–Sat., 10 A.M.–6 P.M. Sun.), a huge high-roller outlet mall with stores such as Calvin Klein, Gap Outlet, Eddie Bauer Outlet, and Adidas to choose among. All told, the complex hosts 45 stores.

Sports and Recreation

The trout in Troutdale is actually the king of trouts, the steelhead. The adjacent Sandy River, which dumps into the Columbia on the outskirts of town, is known as one of the most bountiful steelhead fisheries in the entire state. If you're prepared to brave the icy waters during steelheading's wintery season, try your hand at **Sandy River Delta Park** or **Dabney State Recreation Area.** Pick up tackle, gear and some tips at **Jack's Snack N Tackle** (1208 E. Historic Columbia River Hwy., 503/665-2257, www.jackssnackandtackle.com, 8:30 A.M.–5 P.M. Mon.–Sat.). Or let a guide handle the details so you can concentrate on reeling in the hard-fighting fish. The **Hook Up Guide Service** offers a full- ($175 pp) and half-day ($100) service that includes all equipment and licenses. All you need to do is show up.

Accommodations

Built over a century ago as the county poor farm and old folks' home, the estate at **McMenamins Edgefield** (2126 SW Halsey St., 503/669-8610, www.mcmenamins.com) charms guests with its whimsical play on the 74-acre property's history. Some of the farm land continues to produce veggies and herbs to supply the Edgefield's signature restaurant, the main dormitory has been restored and kitted out as a comfortable lodging house offering a range of European-style rooms, and many other original buildings have been transformed into unique watering holes that serve McMenamins' signature ales. A bit of a theme park for big kids, Edgefield also features two par-three golf courses, a spa, and tons of unique art to spice

up a stroll around the grounds. The accommodations themselves are a lot more comfortable than the property's down-on-its-luck history would lead you to believe, with soft beds and funky furnishings galore. Guests who want a bit more privacy can even choose between a few suites with private baths. Solo travelers will also dig the option of laying up in one of the Edgefield's first-come, first-served hostel beds or reservable twin bed private rooms. Designed to be a bit of an oasis from everyday life, none of the rooms are equipped with TVs or telephones. But then again, given the choices for imbibing around here, the proprietors may well be saving you an embarrassing case of drunk dialing. If you absolutely need it, there's free Wi-Fi in a number of the public areas.

Food

Set up just beyond the century-old Sandy River Bridge along the east bank of the river on the edge of town, **Tad's Chicken 'n' Dumplins** (1325 E. Historic Columbia River Hwy., 503/666-5337, http://tadschicdump.com, 5–10 P.M. Mon.–Fri., 4–10 P.M. Sat.–Sun.) serves stick-to-yer-ribs dinners that make a perfect end-cap to a day exploring the Gorge. With views of the Sandy River through windows draped in red-checkered curtains, Tad's seats you in comfy red vinyl and wood booths. Up-river from that, a bit further outside of town, **Shirley's Tippy Canoe** (28242 E. Historic Columbia River Hwy., 503/492-2220, www .shirleysfood.com, 8 A.M.–8 P.M. daily) sports a huge patio overlooking the Sandy's waters and a long menu of home cookin' served throughout the day.

The nicest restaurant at McMenamins Edgefield, **Black Rabbit Restaurant** (2126 SW Halsey St., 503/492-3086, www.mc menamins.com) serves beautifully presented dishes made with seasonal produce grown on the organic plots scattered across the property's 74 acres.

Information and Services

The **Troutdale Visitor Center** (226 W. Historic Columbia River Hwy., 503/669-7473,

8:30 A.M.–4:30 P.M.) is staffed with friendly and helpful locals who can direct you to the best that the Oregon side of the gorge has to offer with a bundle of maps, brochures, and personal stories.

HISTORIC COLUMBIA RIVER HIGHWAY

The sun-dappled blacktop curves that snake their way east from Troutdale are what the Gorge is best known for. This take-it-slow alternative to I-84 runs parallel to the freeway but higher up on the Gorge's bluffs for unparalleled views. Vista points interrupt the lush canopy here at numerous points along the way, as do a number of impressive waterfalls, including the second-highest year-round waterfall in the States.

Sights
VIEWPOINTS

The **Portland Women's Forum State Scenic Viewpoint** (9 mi. east of Troutdale on Historic Columbia River Highway) presents the first breathtaking view of the Gorge from the vantage of the Historic Columbia River Highway. In the foreground you can see Crown Point with the distinctive Vista House at its tip, while in the distance the ribbon of river snakes its way through basalt walls. The air is redolent with blackberry fragrance in the summer from the vines growing up the hillside here, and if you come in August, you might be able to pick a few to munch while taking in the sights.

If the day is clear and you've got the time, about a half mile east of the Women's Forum overlook, the turnout to Larch Mountain Road will take you 14 miles up to the jaw-dropping panoramic of **Sherrard Viewpoint.** At an elevation of 4,055 feet and with tons of unobstructed views of the Cascades at the picnic area here, on a day with good visibility you can see Mounts St. Helens, Rainier, Adams, Hood, and Jefferson.

VISTA HOUSE AT CROWN POINT

Standing as a beacon of the historic highway on the promontory at Crown Point, Vista House (40700 Historic Columbia River Hwy., 503/695-2230, http://vistahouse.com,

© ERICKA CHICKOWSKI

the view from Vista House at Crown Point

9 A.M.–6 P.M. daily) was conceived when the road was built as "an observatory from which the view both up and down the Columbia could be viewed in silent communion with the infinite." The vistas are definitely worth the stop, but the building itself isn't too shabby, either. Constructed in 1918, this hexagonal Art Nouveau beauty features a beautiful marble rotunda and exterior rock work done by the same Italian masons who crafted the picturesque retaining walls and bridges across the highway. The ruggedly elegant masonry is accented by windows inlaid with green opalized glass and a green tiled roof that complements the palette of the river and surrounding vegetation. The building is a great place to order a latte, make a restroom stop and check out the views from the second-story wraparound veranda before taking on the highway's waterfalls.

◖ GORGE WATERFALLS

Without a doubt, the waterfalls that thunder, cascade, and splash their way down the cliffs beside the Historic Columbia River Highway are the highlight of the drive. The high concentration of falls in the area only makes sense given the geography of the area. With an amazingly active watershed springing up from nearby Mount Hood's glaciers and springs, and a steep embankment of volcanic rock standing between these tributaries and the mighty Columbia, there's only one way for the water to reach its final destination, and that is down, down, down. Lucky for us that it happens in such a dramatic fashion.

The following falls are the most easily accessible along the route, viewable from pull-out areas or short jaunts of under a mile roundtrip. These offer the best sights for the least amount of effort—it's the type of tour you'd feel comfortable taking granny along for. The first stop you'll come across will be a few miles past Corbett, for the faucetlike **Latourell Falls,** which plunges directly down over a columnar basaltic cliff. You can snap plenty of pictures directly from the parking lot or take a 15-minute stroll along a trail from there to get right up to the splash pool.

A bit further down the highway, **Bridal Veil Falls** is a little harder to reach, but worth the 0.6-mile round-trip trek. The only falls that tumble down below the highway, this 118-foot set of tiered horsetail falls is surrounded by mossy cliffs and its own veil of green leaves that make for a pretty snapshot from the viewing platform built across from the bottom tier's splash pool. Parking is ample here and the trail down to the falls is well maintained, but it is not accessible to those with wheelchairs.

But that's OK, because the next few falls offer plenty of ooos and ahhs directly from pavement. Just east of the Bridal Veil parking lot, the lot for **Wahkeena Falls** offers a great look at the cascading gush that gets its name for the Yakama tribe's word for "most beautiful." A short 0.4-mile roundtrip walk to a bridge near the falls will get you close enough to feel the mist coming off of this gushing wonder. And immediately after that on the highway comes the crown jewel of the Gorge's waterfalls, **Multnomah Falls.** Towering almost three times the average height of most of the notable falls in the Gorge area, Multnomah is the second-highest year-round falls in the entire country. With a huge parking lot, a nice restaurant and gift shop on site, and plenty of benches scattered around the paved paths that lead to viewpoints, Multnomah makes for a wonderful afternoon stopover.

The historic highway continues on for another four miles or so east until it joins back up with I-84. Don't be tempted to consider yourself all waterfalled out before heading off the highway—about halfway between Multnomah and the freeway junction, pretty **Horsetail Falls** fans itself over the cliffs just off the highway. Do yourself a favor and at least stop off for a quick peak and a few pics.

Sports and Recreation
WATERFALL HIKES

If you're willing to get out of the car for a while and strap on some sturdy shoes, there are lots of additional waterfall views to be earned by hiking the Forest Service trail system that can be accessed at numerous points along the

© ERICKA CHICKOWSKI

Latourell Falls

highway. Many of these trails can be linked to-gether into gratifying loop hikes. For example, on the west end of the waterfall district, the **Latourell Falls** loop hike is a 2.15-mile loop from the falls parking lot that will take you to an overlook above the main lower falls and past a set of upper falls higher up the creek. The 480-feet of elevation gained by the trail may not seem much on paper but it all comes at once through a steep initial climb on either direction of the route.

Starting from the **Wahkeena Falls** trail-head, a two-mile out-and-back route will take you past numerous upper falls along Wahkeena Creek to the final destination of **Fairy Falls,** a fan-shaped waterfall that can be enjoyed from a hewn log bench at its foot. Along the route, don't miss the very short spur trail to **Lemmon's Viewpoint,** which even surpasses many of those roadside overlooks you thought unbeatable. If you've got the endurance, you can continue past Fairy Falls for a 5.5 mile loop that'll hook east at the Trail 420 junction and back north at the Trail 441 junction past

a pair of out-of-the-way waterfalls, **Ecola Falls** and **Weisendanger Falls,** before taking you down past **Multnomah Falls** and the nearby lodge. A 0.2-mile spur to a great overlook on Multnomah makes for a worthy add-on before continuing down.

From the **Horsetail Falls** parking lot you can set out on a 2.5-mile loop up past its horsetail cousins, **Ponytail Falls** and **Middle Oneonta Falls.** The hike ends with about a half-mile walk along the highway shoulder.

Accommodations

Owned by the original family that built it in 1926, the **Bridal Veil Bed and Breakfast** (across the street from Bridal Veil Falls, 503/695-2333, www.bridalveillodge.com, $139–149) stands as the only lodging estab-lishment right in the Multnomah waterfall dis-trict. Right across the parking lot from Bridal Veil Falls, this antique-laden inn serves full breakfasts that include dishes such as Dutch babies or quiche. Many of the period furnish-ings have been passed down the generations by the family and there's even a photo album featuring post cards to and from the home's first occupants to peruse over coffee.

A midcentury home built using largely recycled materials and to emulate Frank Lloyd Wright's architectural style, **Brickhaven Bed and Breakfast** (38717 E. Historic Columbia River Hwy., 503/695-6326, http://brickhaven. com, $100–125) lies perched upon a hillside overlooking the Gorge, just east of Corbett. All the rooms have views of the river and a public-area sitting room features a heart-stopping panorama from an oversized floor-to-ceiling window.

CAMPING

Set on the easternmost end of the Historic Columbia River Highway, **Ainsworth State Park** (17 mi. east of Troutdale at Exit 35 off of I-84, 503/695-2301, www.orgegonstateparks .org, mid-Mar.–Oct.) offers a range of camping opportunities within day hiking distance to the Multnomah waterfall district. RVers will enjoy the dozens of full hookup sites($20), half of which are pull-through sites to accommodate bigger rigs. There's even a site for campers with disabilities and a handful of walk-in tent sites ($17) for those who'd like to sacrifice amenities for solitude. The campground offers bathrooms with flush toilets and hot showers, and there's an amphitheater that hosts interpretive programs. So what's the catch? Well, all sites are first-come, first-served, so summer planning can be tricky when the throngs arrive.

Food

With big skylights looking up toward Multnomah Falls, the **Multnomah Falls Lodge** (50000 E Historic Columbia River Hwy., 503/695-2676, www.multnomahfallslodge .com, 8 A.M.–9 P.M. daily) dining room feels a bit like an oversized, homey greenhouse. Servers are extra friendly here, always willing to take a snapshot and quick with the orders. Food is fresh and above par compared to other similar destination restaurants, if a bit overpriced. But you're paying for the view, so put a smile on and enjoy it for what it's worth. In the

summer the reservations can get tight, particularly for dinner, so plan ahead. Also, don't be fooled by the name. Though the historic building was originally built for accommodations, this "lodge" only operates as a restaurant.

With so few dining options around these parts, **Corbett Country Market** (36801 E. Historic Columbia River Hwy., 503/695-2234) is a welcome sight for hikers or travelers dying for something to eat or a nice sip of something warm. For the better part of a century, the little country story has been pumping gas and offering up comestibles to road-weary travelers. In addition to coffee, muffins, packaged snacks, and the like, this store sells some delicious homemade beef jerky and local produce.

Information and Services

The U.S. Forest Service runs a **visitors center** at Multnomah Lodge, where you can pick up trail maps, books, and other information about the area.

If you don't plan on taking the scenic route the whole way through from Troutdale, there are a number of access points from I-84 to shortcut your way through to the points that interest you. Exit 22 will bypass the Troutdale and Sandy River areas and deliver you directly to Corbett near the Women's Forum Overlook and the Vista House. Exit 28 will deliver you to the Bridal Veil area and Exit 31 will drop you directly to Multnomah Falls. If you'd like to take the whole route east to west, get off at Exit 35.

Beyond Troutdale, public transit from Portland drops off. If you'd rather enjoy the drive as a passenger, **EcoTours of Oregon** (www.ecotours-of-oregon.com) offers an all-day Columbia River Gorge Waterfalls and Mount Hood Loop Tour for $69.50 per person.

CASCADE LOCKS AND VICINITY

Before the Columbia was tamed through a series of dams, the area around Cascade Locks was a roiling tumble of whitewater that was enough to put gray in the youngest of sailors' beards. The Cascade Rapids descended about 40 feet through a narrow two-mile chute that had to be bypassed by sternwheelers using a locks and canal system that gave the town its name when it was built in 1896. Just over 40 years later, the Bonneville Dam flooded out the rapids and most of the locks, but the town kept its name and still celebrates its early role in river navigation. You can still see a portion of the locks at the town's biggest riverside park, from which a sternwheeler fittingly sets sail each day for a scenic river tour of the Gorge.

Sights
BONNEVILLE DAM
Located four miles west of Cascade Locks, the Oregon side of the Bonneville Dam will give you a look at the dam's first powerhouse and spillway, as well as the dam's navigation locks and the Bonneville Fish Hatchery, which has a big viewing area for steelhead and salmon spawning in the fall, plus a tank that's home to Herman the Sturgeon, an enormous 10-foot, 450-pound white sturgeon who has called the Columbia his home for 70 years. Start your tour at **Bradford Island Visitors Center** (541/374-8820, 9 A.M.–5 P.M. daily, free).

STURGEON

The Columbia River Basin is home to an ancient monster – several thousand, in fact. The white sturgeon is the country's largest freshwater game fish, and it just happens to love the depths below any of the Columbia's dams. Measuring up to 18 feet in length and weighing up to 1,500 pounds, these prehistoric behemoths are often chased by both commercial and recreational fishermen. Check current regulations before wetting a line, and before preheating the oven, bear in mind that these bottom-feeders have plenty of time to soak up toxins over their 100-plus-year lifespan.

HISTORIC LOCKS AND MARINE PARK
Tucked into the manmade watery alcove that made the town what it is today, the **Cascade Locks Marine Park** overlooks remnants of the historic locks that once bypassed Cascade Rapids on the Columbia today. While much of the locks structure was submerged once the Bonneville Dam was built, park visitors can still see evidence of the locks, and just over a pedestrian bridge, serene little **Thunder Island** remains as a byproduct of the canal that was built as part of the 1896 boat-moving project. Today, Thunder Island and the rest of the grounds on the main shore are a great place to take a stroll and enjoy the scenery of passing sailboats and pleasure craft cruising by.

While you're at the park, take a minute to pop in to the **Cascade Locks Historical Museum** (noon–5 P.M. daily May–Sept., free), set inside one of three century-old locks tender's house that stand at the park today. Featuring an old Oregon Pony steam locomotive, memorabilia, artifacts, and photos, the museum provides perspective on the history of the Gorge and the role of sternwheelers and steamboats on the river in the town's bygone era.

If you want to get a little more hands-on with your appreciation of paddleboats, hop aboard the triple-decked sternwheeler **Columbia Gorge** (503/224-3900, www.portlandspirit.com, May–Oct., $28 adult, $18 kids), which boards several times a day from the park. The cruise aboard this craft will present views of the steep basalt cliffs up and down the river during a two-hour narrated tour.

SODERBERG BRONZE
The first bronze foundry opened in the U.S. by a woman, **Soderberg Bronze** (101 Wanapa St., 503/803-9414, www.heathersoderberg.com, 10 A.M.–6 P.M. Thurs.–Mon.) is a studio and foundry run by Heather Soderberg, a one-time child sculpting prodigy and now well-respected artist who sculpted the town's **Sacagawea, Pomp and Seaman** centerpiece over in Marine Park. The foundry offers daily tours. Call ahead for the schedule.

Entertainment and Events

NIGHTLIFE

Throw back a pint, share trail stories with PCT through-hikers, and play a little video poker at the dark and cozy **Pacific Crest Pub** (500 WaNaPa St., 541/374-9310, www.pacificcrestpub.com). Housed in a century-old building, the tavern caters to hikers, offering brochures, maps and other information, and keeping a lively PCT register to chronicle all of the intrepid trekkers who pass by making the Mexico-to-Canada journey.

FESTIVALS AND EVENTS

Held each June, the long-running **Sternwheeler Days** (www.cascadelocks.net/sternwheelerdays) festival at Marine Park celebrates Cascade Locks' riverside history with a sailing regatta and demonstrations from mountain men.

From opening day of boating season in June through its close in September, the locally based **Columbia Gorge Racing Association** (http://cgra.org) hosts a range of sailing regattas and clinics in Cascade Locks.

In early September, the Pacific Crest Trail Association holds **Pacific Crest Trail Days** (www.pcta.org) at Marine Park, where through-hikers gather to camp at Thunder Island, meet old friends they made on the trail, hear about new outdoor products and do a little maintenance on nearby segment of the PCT. Later in September, the **Festival of Nations** (541/553-4883) is a celebration of local Native American heritage that coincides with the spawning of the salmon. Also held at Marine Park, the event hosts children's crafts, tribal performances and a mini-Pow Wow.

Shopping

Featuring a little of this and that right next door to the Pacific Crest Pub, **The Cottage Gifts & Antiques** (502 WaNaPa St., 541/374-5414) sells from a varied collection of art, antiques, and even gemstones. Similarly eclectic, **Lorang Fine Art & Gorge-ous Gifts** (96 WaNaPa St., 541/374-8007, www.lorangfineart.com) displays and sells oil, acrylic, pastel, and watercolor work from 40 different artists, plus wood and basket pieces, Native American masks, glass art, and jewelry. The real highlight of the shop is the owner's steel and bronze sculptures.

Sports and Recreation

HIKING

Across the entire 2,000-plus miles of the **Pacific Crest Trail,** Cascade Locks is the only incorporated town through which the trail runs directly. It's no surprise, then, how many through-hikers take a day or two here to chomp down some burgers, sleep in a fresh bed and pick up a care package before heading over the Bridge of the Gods to tackle the Cascades in Washington. If you're looking to day hike the PCT, the rest stop just south of the bridge makes a great trailhead for a 4.4-mile out-and-back trip along the trail to **Dry Creek Falls.** After about two miles headed southeast from the trailhead, veer right onto Dry Creek Trail to reach the falls. Along the way, you'll come across an old **shoe tree,** which for years has gathered its "fruit" as hikers have tossed their old kicks up in the branches here.

One of the premier hiking trails on either side of the Columbia River Gorge, **Eagle Creek Trail** runs through Northwest rain forests, across impressive footbridges spanning basalt cliffs, and through narrow openings blasted directly into the cliffsides almost a century ago when the historic highway was built nearby. The real draw, though, are the waterfalls. Passing six major waterfalls in six miles, and many more little tumblers and babbling brooks along the way, the stretch is Xanadu for falls fans. For a moderate day hike, try the 4.4-mile round-trip to **Punchbowl Falls.** With only about 400 feet of elevation gain, this satisfying route ends at the 30-foot gusher and passes a viewpoint that overlooks the 100-foot Metlako Falls.

Day hikers with more stamina may want to set their sights on the 12-mile, 1,200-foot gain round-trip to **Tunnel Falls,** a 175-foot plunging falls that uniquely features a trail that was tunneled by dynamite behind the waterfall wall

THE PACIFIC CREST TRAIL

The Pacific Crest Trail, or PCT for those in the know, is really hundreds of trails that link together and run from Mexico all the way up the map to Canada, passing through forests and wilderness far away from civilization. The most dramatic and beautiful part of the trail is the part running through the mountains, rivers, and primordial woods in the state of Washington.

On horseback or on foot, you'd be hard-pressed to find a path that shows off more of Washington than the PCT. Crossing from Oregon, the traveler first comes across The Bridge of the Gods, an awe-inspiring passage across the Columbia River, before beginning a long climb out of the river valley. Then, a long trek through dry lands and ancient lakes leads past the mammoth round top of Mount Adams and across the severe and jagged Goat Rocks Wilderness. Your reward is the unique chance to hike over the Packwood Glacier; small, but a glacier nonetheless.

The trail misses few of the state's highlights, so of course a section skirting Mount Rainier is mandatory. A long stretch through the mysterious North Cascades full of old-growth trees and deep, clear lakes follows, leading the hiker deeper and deeper until he or she arrives at remote Lake Chelan. From there, things only get wilder approaching the border. The hiker or equestrian passes through the rugged, mountainous Pasayten Wilderness toward the ultimate payoff: views of hundreds of glaciers and year-round snowfields. A little farther leads to Monument 78, the Canadian border, and a deep sense of peace and a well-deserved sense of accomplishment. And hopefully a good rest before taking the long way back home.

and then on a blasted ledge halfway up the cliff where the water shoots over. This trail can also be backpacked, though the competition for the limited sites along the way is fierce in summer months. Hikers who choose to turn it in to a multiday loop will find that the trail syncs up with the PCT after 13.3 miles at Wahtum Lake and back down Benson Plateau to the trailhead on **Ruckel Creek Trail** for a total of almost 27 miles. To reach the Eagle Creek trailhead, take exit 41 off of I-84 eastbound and follow the road east until it ends a mile later. The exit only comes off the eastbound lanes, so if you are coming from Hood River, you'll need to take exit 40 and backtrack east a mile to the next exit. Parking at the trailhead requires a $5 Northwest Forest Pass.

HISTORIC COLUMBIA RIVER HIGHWAY STATE TRAIL

Extend your appreciation for the winding, scenic curves of the historic highway that much of I-84 replaced by walking or cycling the Historic Columbia River Trail. Oregon State Parks administers a couple of disconnected sections of pavement restored from some of the abandoned parts of the highway, one of which runs west from the parking lot at the Bridge of the Gods five miles over to Moffett Creek. With moss and shaded wildflowers decorating the path and views of the river and Bonneville Dam, this is a class act spot for a spin.

BOATING AND FISHING

The exposed concrete left over from the canal and locks over at **Marine Park** make for a popular fishing pier these days. The water flowing through this manmade feature seems to attract an ample supply of fish and the park features a fish cleaning station near the restrooms. The park also sports two boat launches for those who want to venture further out in the river. The adjacent marina features free moorage and dump station facilities for up to 72 hours. If you need to pick up tackle, bait, or even a fancy new rod, check out **Columbia Action Custom Rods** (502 WaNaPa St., 541/374-5414).

Accommodations and Camping

Perched along the river just east of the Bridge of

the Gods, **Best Western Plus Columbia River Inn** (735 WaNaPa St., 541/374-8777, $130 d) hosts the best digs in town. Meticulously clean with fresh furnishings and a whirlpool tub and pool facility, it'll satisfy most road-trippers. Ask for a riverside room with a balcony to soak up the view. Just be aware that the scenery comes with a caveat: the hotel overlooks the river *and* the railroad tracks that run above it. Light sleepers may not be fans, but kids will love the choo-choos and the housekeepers at least provide earplugs alongside the conditioner and shampoo bottles each day.

For a slightly cheaper alternative, **Bridge of the Gods Motel and RV Park** maintains a collection of motel rooms ($69–119) and self-contained cabins ($119–149) in its log-cabin-style buildings. Both options come equipped with kitchenettes, jetted tubs, and free Wi-Fi, and the property also has laundry facilities on site to clean up those rain and waterfall-soaked hiking clothes. The grounds also host RV overnight spots, but there are nicer camping options in town. The best bet is at **Marine Park Campground** ($25 hookups, $15 tent), right in the city's pride and joy park. The small campground offers a handful of sites with water and electric hookups, showers, and a dump station. There's a playground on the property, free Wi-Fi and even a book exchange. Best yet, the waterfront location can't be beat. For a bit more serenity, tent campers and RVers with small rigs who can do without hookups may prefer **Herman Creek Campground** (Frontage Rd. and Herman Creek Rd., $10) on the eastern outskirts of town. This Forest Service site offers a quiet stay under a piney canopy, with water spigots and vault toilets. The site is a trailhead for several routes, including the Pacific Crest Trail. The site doubles as a horse camp, so PCT riders can bring their horse trailers and steeds here.

Food

For the best hunk o' ground beef this side of Hood River and a fantastic view of the river and the Bridge of the Gods, **Charburger** (745 NW WaNaPa St., 541/374-8477) is the place

to go. To fill the limited dining options of the area, this burger stand also runs a bakery, cooks up a number of breakfast items, lays out a salad bar during lunch and dinner, and even serves lighter fare such as salmon burgers to sate calorie counters.

East Wind Drive-In (395 NW WaNaPa St., 541/374-8380) also does burgers, but the big neon sign of a penguin hefting an oversized cone should be your cue to where the real priorities are here. When the sun's shining, nothing beats a sweet treat from East Wind.

Information and Services

Get information about Marine Park and the rest of the town's amenities at **Port of Cascade Locks.** The steady stream of boot-clad backpackers streaming through the doors at the **Cascade Locks Post Office** are PCT through-hikers who like to mail food ahead here to help them finish the rest of their journey up in Washington. Check out the PCT register at the post office to sign in or look at who's been hiking by here. Hikers can also find pay showers at the **Marine Park Campground.**

HOOD RIVER

The central hub of recreation and repast in the Columbia Gorge, Hood River is at once sophisticated and homespun. "The Hood" is home to way more than its fair share of amazing restaurants for a town of its size, attracting culinary talent with its backdoor proximity to quality farms, orchards, and vineyards and its strong concentration of local microbreweries and wineries. At the same time, locals never take themselves too seriously and you'll never get an uptight vibe in town.

You can probably credit that to the fun mix of growers and outdoor enthusiasts who live here and share a love for the natural beauty of the Gorge and Mount Hood around them. Many farmers and orchardists have lived off of bountiful Hood River Valley harvests for generations. At the same time, recreation junkies have for decades been drawn to the Hood for the area's perfect combination of weather and geography. At the nexus of the Columbia River

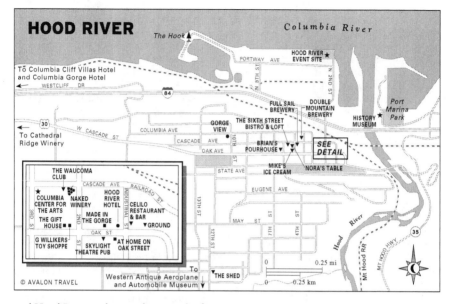

and Hood River, and just an hour north of Mt. Hood, the town is a perfect jumping off point for natural exploration by bike, boat, board, or boot. The sizzling summers invite the active set to get wet, and the blustery wind tunnel created by the Gorge here has contributed to make this the windsurfing and kiteboarding capital of the world. Meanwhile, in winter the consistent layer of powder on Mount Hood and its foothills prompts skiers to break out the bindings and wax for downhill and cross-country action.

Sights
WESTERN ANTIQUE AEROPLANE AND AUTOMOBILE MUSEUM
Known around town simply as WAAAM (1600 Air Museum Road, 541/308-1600, www.waaamuseum.com, 9 A.M.–5 P.M. daily, $12 adults, $10 seniors and veterans, $6 students, free children 4 and under and active military), this repository of antique machines that go "vroom" is sure to rev any gearhead's engine. With a collection of 75 aircraft, including a 1917 Curtiss JN4D Jenny, WAAAM's flying history primarily spans the early two decades of flight. In addition, you can find over 100 autos and

military jeeps, including a 1914 Ford Model T Depot Hack, several Model As and early Dodge, Mercury, and Studebaker cars.

THE HISTORY MUSEUM AT HOOD RIVER
The town's historical museum (300 E. Port Marina Dr., 541/386-6772, 10 A.M.–4 P.M. Mon.–Sat., noon–4 P.M. Sun. Apr.–Aug., noon–4 P.M. daily Sept.–Oct., $3 adults, free kids 10 and under and military) displays a range of permanent exhibits that includes dolls from pioneers in the valley, Native American beadwork and basketry, and artifacts that offer a look into over a century of history in Hood River Valley.

FRUIT LOOP
The bountiful orchard rows, rustic barns, putt-putting tractors, and farm dogs of the Hood River Valley lie in the shadow of Mount Hood, making the valley's back roads some of the most scenic in all of the Northwest. The locals affectionately refer to the 35-mile loop of Highway 35 running south and connecting down in Parkdale with Dee Highway 281 as the Fruit Loop. All along the route, participating farms, orchards, fruit stands, and more

invite visitors to their grounds to take pictures, sample products, and pet animals. A fold-out brochure featuring information on more than 30 stops on the loop is abundantly available in town. The following are a few of the best things to see and do along the route.

Come watch furry alpacas scamper and lounge in their paddocks at **Cascade Alpacas** (4207 Sylvester Dr., 541/354-3542, www .foothillsyarn.com, 11 A.M.–4 P.M. Sat.–Sun. Mar., 11 A.M.–4 P.M. Fri.–Sun. Apr.–May and Nov.–Dec. 18, 11 A.M.–5 P.M. daily June– Oct.). These long-necked cuties are prized for their extremely soft wool and their friendly dispositions compared to their South American cousin, the llama. On the property you can get your hands on skeins of that wool, plus scarves, hats, socks, and sweaters made from the stuff.

Just a few minutes from downtown, **Wilinda Blueberry Patch** (730 Frankton Rd., 801/556-7964, 9 A.M.–6 P.M. daily July–Labor Day) opens its blueberry field to u-pickers between July and Labor Day. The patch grows a number of blueberry varieties that ripen at different times throughout that two-month window.

Visit **Lavender Valley Lavender Farm** (3925 Portland Dr., 541/386-1906, www .lavendervalley.com, 10 A.M.–6 P.M. daily June–Labor Day, 10 A.M.–5 P.M. Thurs.–Sun. Sept., 11 A.M.–4 P.M. Sat.–Sun. Oct.) in July to catch the lavender bloom at its peak for incredible pictures of purple fields backdropped by the imposing glaciers of Mount Hood. Open April through October, the farm runs a u-cut operation when in bloom, allowing visitors to pick from 70 varieties of lavender straight from the field. The rest of the months, enjoy the art gallery featuring hand-painted glass and get a whiff of the lavender oil that's distilled on the property in the late summer and fall.

More than just a fruit stand, **Mountain View Orchards** (6670 Trout Creek Ridge Rd., 541/352-6554, www.mtvieworchards.com, 9 A.M.–5 P.M. daily mid-July–Oct.) usually has enough activities on the property to keep the typical family busy for a good couple of hours. The owners have built three hiking trails on

© ERICKA CHICKOWSKI

Mount Hood rises above Hood River.

© ERICKA CHICKOWSKI

The petting zoo at Draper Girls Country Farm is a hit with the younger set.

the property for folks to explore, frequently run tours, host hayrides on the weekends, and put together a full slate of events during the month of October. The bakery on the property serves pie à la mode and runs a cider mill for fresh-pressed cider. And, unsurprisingly, the orchard offers u-pick apples, pears, peaches, cherries, pumpkins, and corn, depending on the season.

U-pick enthusiasts with a soft spot for farm animals may also want to consider stopping by **Draper Girls Country Farm** (6200 Hwy. 35, 541/352-6625, www.drapergirlscountry farm.com). In addition to u-pick of fruit by the bushel, and a store with some amazing jams and fruit butters, Draper Girls has a petting zoo featuring sheep, goats, pigs, and more.

Set up on a side road right along the Fruit Loop route, **Glassometry Studios** (3015 Lower Mill Dr., 541/354-3015, www.glass ometry.com) gives intrepid visitors the opportunity to feel the heat of the kiln with a special four-hour hands-on workshop ($200 pp for two, $180 pp for four). Even if you don't plan to work in the studio, the shop's artists

display a pretty glass garden outside and sell their wares from a store that features windows looking into the work area.

MOUNT HOOD SCENIC RAILROAD

If you've already been cooped up in the car long enough, skip the Fruit Loop drive and see the Hood River Valley by train instead. Take the excursion train from the town of Hood River 22 miles all the way down to its terminus in Parkdale for a four-hour round-trip tour. Or do a two-hour trip to Odell. On some weekends the railroad spices rides up with a Western Train Robbery–themed train great for kids who want to help be on the lookout for train robbers who'll try to stop the train to carry out their old-timey larceny. Mount Hood Scenic Railroad also offers a number of brunch and dinner excursions within its equipped dining cars, including a very fun Murder Mystery Dinner Train.

VIEWPOINTS

There are a number of tripod-friendly places in and around Hood River to take in panoramic views of the Gorge and Mount Hood. At the little Ruthton Park, **Ruthton Point Overlook** (0.4 mile west of Columbia Gorge Hotel on Westcliff Dr.) presents a view of Ruthton Point and Washington cliffs in the distance, as well as passing trains as they snake their way just below at river level. And at **Panorama Point County Park,** clear days will give you vistas of Mount Hood towering over the orchards and vineyards of the fertile Hood River Valley. The park is only about three miles out of the central downtown district. Just take State Route 35 south to Eastside Road, take a left, and follow the signs to the park.

FULL SAIL BREWERY TOUR

The driving force behind Hood River's heritage as the microbrewery mecca in the Gorge region, Full Sail Brewery has been concocting its suds by the Columbia since 1989. A beloved institution among the boardheads, farmers, and even vintners in the Hood, Full Sail throws open its brewery doors for an informative half-hour tour four times a day. The guides will show you the equipment and the fresh ingredients that go into the beer that goes out the door and will tell you about how the upstart brewery started here out of a defunct fruit cannery. The tour ends in the Full Sail Tasting Room, where you can give most of its stock a sip for $1.

WINERIES

Set up right next to the Mount Hood Scenic Railroad depot, **Springhouse Cellar's** casual tasting bar is driven by a unique innovation: wine on tap. Committed to sustainable winemaking, Spinghouse serves up a red and a white wine stored within its old cannery building cellar upstairs via a unique tap system that gives the winery the ability to offer wine refills to anyone who comes with a cleaned out, empty wine bottle in hand. The winery isn't just about schtick, though, serving some delicious wines from bottles as well. Try the surprisingly complex Cherry Ort or the house specialty Ruins Red, a sangiovese/merlot/cab blend named after the old remnants of a distillery on the property.

Just a few minutes from downtown, the tasting room at **Cathedral Ridge Winery** is run out of a little cottage flanked by vineyard rows and a grassy picnic area bedecked with old barrels full of flowers and an incredible view of Mount Adams to the north. Inside, the wines take center stage, serving with some of the best reds south of the Columbia. The reserve syrah and the reserve cabernet are worth the trip all by themselves.

Focused primarily on Italian varietals, **Marchesi Vineyards** goes all out to embrace its owner's Italian winemaking heritage in the tasting room. Expect a warm reception, red checkered cloths, a mural imported from Italy's Piedmonte growing district and some Italian olive trees outside on the patio to complete the effect. The winery's sangiovesi and experimental dolcetto are both the highlights of this tasting stop along the Fruit Loop.

With a bar featuring ornately carved accents and giant mirrors, a dramatically high ceiling and huge windows with sweeping views of its vineyards and Mount Hood in the skyline, **Mt. Hood Winery** runs one of the classiest tasting rooms in the entire Hood River Valley. With vines growing on a 100-year-old farm along the

© ERICKA CHICKOWSKI

the tasting room at Mt. Hood Winery

Fruit Loop that still tends an impressive pear orchard, the wine here often features fruity flavors that are imparted through soil long used to apples, cherries, and pears. Try the pinot noir, or for something unique, the pear wine stands as a sweet but extremely crisp summer wine.

For a whirlwind tour of the best wines the Gorge has to offer, stop at **The Gorge White House** on your way back from the Fruit Loop. The said house is a century-old Dutch Colonial home on a farm with an equally long heritage. It's been converted inside to a tasting room that serves more than 30 wines from a smattering of local vintners, plus tastes of local microbrews. While you're there, you can venture out into the farm's u-cut flower fields to pick out a bouquet for that special someone.

Entertainment and Events
NIGHTLIFE

Enjoy live music most weekends from the stage at **Wacouma Club** (207 Cascade Ave., 541/387-2583, www.waucomaclub.com, 4 P.M.–2 A.M. Mon.–Fri., 9 A.M.–2 A.M. Sat.–Sun.), an established stop for local bands in the area, who come to play the small stage at this cozy joint. You can also take a seat at its long wooden bar on Tuesday nights to enjoy the rhythms played soulfully at its weekly blues jam session.

A serious winery with a cheeky name, **Naked Winery & Orgasmic Wine Company** frequently hosts bands on the weekends and competes with Wacouma through its own Tuesday evening jazz nights.

A movie house at a pizzeria? Yes indeedy. **Skylight Theatre Pub** screens first-run movies from its digs inside Andrew's Pizza, letting audiences enjoy a pie and some local beers while being thrilled and chilled. That's a mite better than popcorn and Jujubees, don't you think?

If you're looking to rub elbows with the hard-charging boardheads, mountain bikers, and other long-time locals, motor south of downtown to the out of the way establishment **The Shed.** A no-nonsense spot equipped with booths and video poker machines, The Shed serves a mean cocktail and offers a pool table to while the night away.

THE COLUMBIA CENTER FOR THE ARTS

An institution in the Hood for over three decades, Columbia Arts Stage Troup, or **CAST,** presents plays, musicals, dance performances, and concerts out of the Columbia Center for the Arts (215 Cascade St., 541/387-8877, www.columbiaarts.org). In addition, the venue hosts lectures and films and runs an art gallery (11 A.M.–5 P.M. Wed.–Sun.) heavy on local talent.

FESTIVALS AND EVENTS

From May through October, many businesses in downtown Hood River band together to host a fun **First Friday** event. On the first Friday of each month, stores stay open late, run specials, host music and activities, and feature art and gifts tailored for the strong out-of-towner contingent visiting during the warmer months.

Strong swimmers can put themselves to the ultimate test on Labor Day, when Hood River plays host to the **Roy Webster Cross-Channel Swim.** The event ferries out a group of cap-and-goggled freestylers to the other side of the Columbia River and deposits them in the water to swim 1.1 miles across and back to Hood River. It's a challenging, chaotic field, often with 500 or more sets of swim caps, arms, and legs churning the water to reach the shore.

For close to 60 years, Hood River Valley has celebrated the annual bloom on its fruit trees during April's **Blossom Fest** (541/386-2000, http://hoodriver.org/blossom-fest). The events tied to the fest range from a Craft Show to a fire department all-you-can-eat-breakfast, with little mini-shindigs across the valley. This is the prime time to drive the Fruit Loop, with many of the stops on the route participating with activities on their properties.

Held each year on the first Saturday of October, **Hops Fest** honors its prime beer-making crop with an event centered around the ales, ambers, porters, and more that have brought the Gorge so much fame as a craft brewing capital in the States. Expect to have the hop-portunity to try dozens of different beers, many of them specially brewed to feature the distinctive taste of freshly harvested hops.

In mid-October, **Harvest Fest** marks the end of growing season for the Hood River Valley. Shop for fresh fruits and veggies at Produce Row, which offers up delights like Anjou pears, heirloom apples, pumpkins, and roasted nuts. Participate in an annual pie-eating contest, take a horse-drawn carriage ride, enjoy live music, or just get your fill tasting delicacies like artisan jams, chocolate-covered nuts, and smoked salmon for sale.

In December Hood River is frequently blanketed with a light layer of snow, making perfect scenery for the month-long slate of events during **Hood River Holidays.** Things are typically kicked off the first weekend of the month with a holiday parade down Oak Street and the lighting of downtown twinklers. Throughout the month wineries usually offer special tastings, Santa can be found frequently at downtown Santaland, and Mount Hood Railroad runs a special Polar Express train through the valley.

Shopping

With its cute collection of mom-and-pop boutiques and gift shops tucked into historic buildings, downtown Hood River's Oak Street is a vacation shopper's ideal walkway, filled with window shopping and souvenirs.

Featuring furnishing and unique decor items, **At Home on Oak Street** sells a unique smattering of accents surely not to be replicated by neighbors back home. Nearby, **Made in the Gorge** (108 Oak St., 541/386-2830, www.madeinthegorge.com, 10 A.M.–5 P.M. daily) displays a well-rounded mix of jewelry, painting, pottery, and sculpture created by local artists from in and around Hood River.

For more conventional tourist T-shirts, novelty gift snacks, and other souvenir baubles, **The Gift House** (204 Oak St., 541/386-9234, www.hoodrivergifthouse.com) has your bases covered. Pick up smoked salmon, chocolate-covered huckleberries, or fresh jam without having to take a drive out on the Fruit Loop. And kids and the young at heart will find a stop at **G Willikers Toy Shoppe** (202 Oak St., 541/387-2229, 10 A.M.–6 P.M. Mon.–Sat.,

10 A.M.–5 P.M. Sun.) to be mandatory. This toy store sells a wide range of games, stuffed animals, books, educational items, and other quality playthings that only the best elves on Santa's production line are put in charge of.

Sports and Recreation
WINDSURFING AND KITEBOARDING
The undisputed hub of wind-borne watersports in the Gorge, Hood River draws self-proclaimed boardheads from around the world, who flock here to ply the windy and scenic waters of the Columbia. Also known as sailboarding, windsurfing is powered by a mount that looks like a cross between a surfboard and a sailboat. An extreme sport around these parts for decades, sailboarding will always remain in vogue to some degree, but of late it has been supplanted in the hearts of many of the Gorge's adrenaline junkies by kiteboarding. Also referred to as kitesurfing, this high-octane sport sends enthusiasts careening over the water on a wakeboardlike mount powered by a line attached to a large C-shaped sail.

Both are technical sports that'll take some degree of education and training to get started. Fortunately Hood River has the highest concentration of schools for both in the entire country. If you take a lesson in town, more likely than not you'll be meeting at either the **Hood River Sailpark** (300 E. Port Marina Dr.) or the **Hood River Event Site** (north end of 2nd St. off of I-84 exit 63) each on either side of the Hood River outlet into the Columbia and both popular launch sites for boardheads of all experience levels. Try Hood River WaterPlay for a range of windsurfing lessons that run the gamut from a Quick Start two-hour ($69) lesson to a full two-day, six-hour U.S. Sailing sanctioned windsurf class ($199) that affords you free time on the company's equipment at its beginner beach throughout the sailing season after graduation. Meanwhile, for kiteboarding, the Port of Hood River has sanctioned six different outfits to teach classes from local launch spots. Located at a stand over at the Event Site, **New Wind Kite School** (541/387-2440) runs an individualized full-day

SURFING THE WIND

Because the Columbia is the only major break in the Cascade Range, it acts as an 80-mile-long wind tunnel. The wind blowing through the Columbia Gorge provides some of the best windsurfing and kiteboarding conditions in the nation. In 1991, a windsurfer set the national speed record, 47.4 miles per hour, here. This place isn't for beginners: gusty winds, large waves, a strong current, and frigid water make the Gorge challenging for even experienced sailors, and the constant parade of tugs and barges adds more hazards. Winds average 16 mph between March and mid-October, but most surfers and boarders prefer to come in July and August when the water is warmer and the current is slower.

The most protected waters in the Gorge are at Vancouver Lake near Vancouver, and at Horsethief Lake near the Dalles bridge, but here strong winds may make it difficult for the beginner to return to the upwind launch area. A good place to learn is The Dalles Riverfront Park, just across the river in Oregon, where you can take lessons and rent equipment in a relatively protected location. Board rentals are also available in Stevenson and Bingen, Washington, and Hood River, Oregon. If you just want to watch, the best place is near the Spring Creek Fish Hatchery three miles west of Bingen, where you may see upwards of 300 boarders on a windy August day.

Several good places for intermediate-level boarders are near Stevenson, Home Valley, Bingen, and Avery Park (east of Horsethief Lake). Avery Park is especially good because it has a long, straight stretch of river that gets nicely formed waves.

Expert-level conditions can be found at Swell City, four miles west of the Bingen Marina; the Fish Hatchery, 3.5 miles west of White Salmon; Doug's Beach, 2.5 miles east of Lyle; Maryhill State Park, where the river is less than a half mile wide; and the east end of the river near Roosevelt Park. Experts head to The Wall, 1.5 miles east of Maryhill State Park.

For general information on the sport, contact the Columbia Gorge Windsurfing Association (541/386-9225, www.cgwa.net) in Hood River, Oregon.

More than 50 sites provide access on both sides of the Columbia River; check with local shops for details. For up-to-date wind conditions, listen to radio stations 104.5 FM and 105.5 FM, or check with windsurfing shops in Hood River, Oregon – the center of the windsurfing universe. On the Web, head to www.windance.com for live Gorge "windcams" and weather updates. Showers are available at the Lyle Merc store or the Bingen School Inn.

Introduction to Kiteboarding for 1–2 people ($254–320 pp), as well as a two-day Fast Track Camp ($414 pp) for two that will really get you jump-started by getting you out on the water quickly through Jet Ski–assisted lessons.

VIENTO STATE PARK

One of the premier plots of state park land along the Gorge lies about eight miles west of Hood River. The aptly named Viento—in Spanish it means "wind"—brings together some beautiful riverfront property that sprawls south past the freeway into the waterfall-laden scenery the Oregon side of the Gorge is known for. On the river, windsurfers and kiteboarders take advantage of convenient access to launch their rigs. And for tumbling water, take the one-mile, fully accessible paved trail to the Starvation Creek waterfall along a now-defunct section of the Historic Columbia River Highway.

KOBERG BEACH
STATE RECREATION SITE

Just a couple miles east of Hood River, Koberg Beach was the town's go-to riverfront site when it was a tony little resort for most of the first half of the 20th century. The resort is gone but the beach along the Columbia remains a favorite place to recreate, with wind-sport enthusiasts and anglers taking full advantage of easy river access. The beach is conveniently right off of I-84, but the towering basaltic **Stanley Rock** keeps freeway noise down to a minimum.

MOUNTAIN BIKING
Mountain bikers will find a little something for every riding style and ability among the spaghettilike collection of trails curving through **Post Canyon** just south of town. Twisting and turning through land owned by the Hood River County Forestry Department, these shared use trails extend out to 89 miles of exploration from multiple staging areas, but Post Canyon is the most popular with the mountain biker set. To get there, take Country Club road for 1.4 miles from Oak Street and turn right onto Post Canyon Road for about half a mile until it turns to gravel. You can park there and ride another 1.2 miles up the road to the first trailhead, or chance it with your car along the bumpy road to see if the limited parking at the end of the road isn't full.

The quintessential ride in the Hood River region lies on the 11.7-mile **Surveyor's Ridge** trail, a demanding and serpentine line of singletrack that's most frequently ridden as a shuttle-ride. With more than 2,000-feet in elevation gain, much of it in very steep sections leading up and along the ridgeline that offers incredible views of Mount Hood and the Hood River Valley. To reach the trailhead from the south end, take State Route 35 26 miles from Hood River to Forest Service Road 44. Take a left and follow that for 3.5 miles to Road 620. The trail crosses it just a few yards away. From the north end, take Highway 35 south for 14 miles and turn left on Pine Mont Drive. Follow it five miles to Road 630, where you'll take a right and follow it to the parking area.

To get info on these and other local trails, pick up spare tubes and parts or rent a bike, check out **Discover Bicycle** (210 State St., 541/386-4820, http://discoverbicycles.com, 10 A.M.–6 P.M. Mon.–Sat., 10 A.M.–5 P.M. Sun.).

WHITEWATER RAFTING
Take a tumbling and scenic ride on the town's namesake waterway with **Northwest Rafting**

Company (116 Oak St., Ste. 4, 541/450-9855, www.nwrafting.com, $135) on its full-day Hood River whitewater rafting tour. Starting in the exciting Class II and Class IV rapids of the river's West Fork, the ride calms down through the bucolic Hood River Valley for some beautiful views. Lunch is held near Punchbowl Falls and the ride floats its way all the way back right into town.

Accommodations
You can't beat the convenient location of **Hood River Hotel** (102 Oak St., 541/386-1900 or 800/386-1859, www.hoodriverhotel.com, $89 and up), an old brick hotel set downtown right in the mix of Oak Street's shops and restaurants. Rooms are a bit cramped, but the property features cheap parking ($5), a fitness center with sauna and whirlpool tub, free wireless and accepts pets in some rooms. Snag a suite for more space to spread out and a fully equipped kitchen or kitchenette.

Fans of historic hotels will probably enjoy **Columbia Gorge Hotel** (4000 Westcliff Dr., 541/386-5566 or 800/345-1921, www.columbiagorgehotel.com, $159 and up) better. First gaining prominence in the era of the Historic Columbia River Highway's heyday, this stately lodge overlooks an impressive rocky Gorge vista from its bluffside position. Furnishings, wallpaper, and art all hearken back to a rose-colored time when the establishment played host to bigwigs like Presidents Roosevelt and Coolidge, Rudolph Valentino, and Jane Powell. In the lobby an elevator operator runs a turn of the century lift and you'll spot floral patterns and intricate moldings galore. Of course, like many historic accommodations, this one comes with the floorboard creaks and temperamental plumbing as part of the package. But the views and ambiance contribute to a fun experience. The hotel exterior and grounds are accented by a barrel-tiled roof and mason work done by the same Italian craftsmen who worked on the highway bridges and the Vista House on Crown Point. These features are complemented by carefully tended and colorful gardens and there are ample viewpoints on the grounds to watch the river take its course. There's even a gushing 200-foot waterfall on the property. It's worth a visit even if you don't intend to stay there.

If you like the waterfall and grounds but prefer a newer establishment, the adjacent **Columbia Cliff Villas** (3880 Westcliff Dr., 541/436-2660 or 866/912-8366, $169 and up) should be a good fit. Featuring the same dramatic Gorge views and sharing the grounds and spa amenities with the Columbia Gorge Hotel, the sparkling new condo buildings of the Villas all come with flat screen TVs, coffee makers, and plush beds. Many rooms have gas fireplaces and spacious river-view patios. There are also many multibedroom suite options with full kitchens, making this a pleasing place to set up larger families. Decor is casual elegance, with granite and marble accents in the kitchens and bathrooms, and fine linens and furnishing throughout. The property offers free Wi-Fi, nanny services, room service, and in-room spa treatments to round out the amenities.

The meals are deliciously filling and the conversation convivial around the breakfast table at **Seven Oaks Bed and Breakfast** (1373 Barker Rd., 541/386-7622, www.sevenoaks bb.com, $160 d). Owned by an energetic couple who raised their kids in Hood River and have an intimate familiarity with the area, the inn is run out of a pretty Craftsman home with a porch and swing facing a lush lawn and nicely tended garden. A few minutes away from Hood River's central district, Seven Oaks strikes a delicate balance of convenience and country ambiance. The grounds here sport a great big barn with a chicken coop, awesome views of Mounts Hood and Adams and a sun deck with a whirlpool tub. Not a stitch of lace or frou-frou floral patterns will clutter up your rooms here. Just crisp, white linens, an incredibly soft mattress, and early American furnishings to add a little flavor to the tasteful decor.

Just one block off of downtown's Oak Street and within walking distance to some of the area's best pubs, the porch wrapping around the Victorian-style house at **Gorge View** (1009 Columbia St., 541/386-5770, http://gorgeview .com, $85–95) bed-and-breakfast overlooks the mighty Columbia and Mount Adams. Catering

Catch a quiet night's rest at Seven Oaks Bed and Breakfast.

© ERICKA CHICKOWSKI

to the outdoor enthusiast crowd, Gorge View offers plenty of storage space to hold your sporting gear and serves a hearty morning breakfast in its country-style dining room.

Resting in a vibrant Hood River Valley farm and orchard with a breathtaking view of Mount Hood, **Sakura Ridge** (5601 York Hill Dr., 877/472-5872, http://sakuraridge.com) is tucked between rows of fruit trees and gentle pastures dotted with sheep and lamb. Bedecked in natural wood siding, the Sakura lodge hosts large rooms with private baths, most featuring private decks that face the mountain. Breakfast highlights the fruit of the farm's harvest, featuring fresh herbs and produce and eggs straight from the property's chicken coop.

CAMPING

Open mid-March through October, **Viento State Park** runs a first-come, first-serve campsight featuring 56 RV sites with electric and water hookups and an additional 18 sites just for tenters. The RV loop offers great access to the river, but its proximity to the busy railroad tracks that run through the park may disturb light sleepers, especially from sites A1 through A31.

Tenters looking for a quieter spot closer to town may prefer **Tucker Park** (five mi. south of Hood River on Hwy. 281, 541/386-4477), situated right along the waters of Hood River. You'll find 94 tent sites ($18 normal, $22 riverside) and a handful of RV sites with water hookups ($19). Again, this spot doesn't accept reservations.

RV campers who want to lock in a spot at a park with amenities may want to head across the Hood River Bridge, where on the Washington side there lies a very convenient spot named the **Bridge RV Park and Campground** (652714 SR 14, 509/493-1111, www.bridgerv.com).

Food
CAFÉS AND BAKERIES

A reimagining of the classic diner, coffee-shop-style, **Ground Espresso Bar and Cafe** (12 Oak St., 541/386-4442, http://groundhoodriver.com, 6 A.M.–4 P.M. daily) is bedecked in decor featuring midcentury touches like plastic bucket seats, hula girl wall hangings, and an orange and brown motif. In addition to the lattes and cappuccinos, you can get yourself a beer or wine and the food presents a tasty mix of fresh pastries and breakfast sandwiches, paninis, salads, and smoothies.

PUB GRUB

It's a raucous scene inside **Brian's Pourhouse's** (606 Oak St., 541/387-4344, www.brianspourhouse.com, 5 A.M.–11 P.M. daily, main courses $15–22) little white clapboard house, fitting for one of Hood River's few late-night dining establishments. Its seasonal menu is built around bold flavors, with a handful of salads and small plates complementing stick-to-your-rib entrées like hanger steak and grilled lamb sirloin. Brian's also offers several pub favorites like burgers, pizza, and its house-specialty fish tacos.

With a similarly effervescent atmosphere, **Double Mountain Brewery Taproom** (8 4th St., 541/387-0042, 4–11 P.M. Tues.–Thurs., 11:30 A.M.–11 P.M. Fri.–Mon.) lays out a varied menu but the real attraction is its brick-oven pizza. Baked up fast in a super-hot oven, this is East Coast–style pizza with nice bits of char on the crust and plenty of gooey cheese. Pizza snobs, I dare you to turn your nose up at this pick—it's good enough to compete with arguably the best microbrew selection created in the Hood.

Hands-down, though, **Full Sail Tasting Room and Pub** (506 Columbia St., 541/386-2247, 11:30 A.M.–10 P.M. daily) offers the best overall menu and the nicest atmosphere for families—particularly during the lunch hours. Try the special Full Sail Burger with smoked gouda and caramelized onions or go with a healthier but quite delicious turkey and brie. And don't forget dessert—several unique sweets feature Full Sail beer as ingredients, including the unique Session Black Float with ice cream dolloped into a glass of black lager.

CONTEMPORARY NORTHWEST

A high-class restaurant that could easily compete with the best Seattle or Portland has to offer, **Celilo Restaurant and Bar** (16 Oak St., 541/386-5710, www.celilorestaurant.com, 11:30 A.M.–3 P.M. and 5–9 P.M. Mon.–Sat., 9 A.M.–3 P.M. and 5–9 P.M. Sun., $14–24) creates a warm and classy atmosphere with a dining room done up in honey-colored maple-wood and earth-tone fabrics, low lighting, and an attentive staff at your call to serve amid it all. The food is the real show-stopper. A daring mix of seasonal fare creatively presented, Celilo's rotating menu fixates on the fruit and veggies grown in Hood Valley, paired with the chef's delicate sauces and seasonings. Menu picks featuring the hanger steak are a dependable choice here.

Nibblers will delight at the small plate selection at **◖ Nora's Table** (110 5th St., 541/387-4000, www.norastable.com, 5–9 P.M. Tues.–Thurs, 5–10 P.M. Fri.–Sat.), a laid-back but gourmand café that speaks the language of local—ingredients are freshly plucked from the proverbial back door. Just about everything is house-made, even the pickles, the ketchup, and the beer crackers. If the scallops are on the menu, drop all competing plans and order them. Plump and crispy on the outside with the melt-in-your-mouth middles, these are the shellfish of your daydreams.

You'll have quite a decision to make at **The Sixth Street Bistro and Loft** (6th St. and Cascade Ave., 541/386-5737, 11:30 A.M.–9:30 P.M. Sun.–Thurs., 11:30 A.M.–10 P.M. Fri.–Sat., $8–16), which plates up plenty of epicurean choices but also grills up the best burger in town. Whether you choose the Damn Good Cheeseburger or a colorful salad, you'll be able to enjoy it on the nicest patio on town, which sits on a quiet downtown side street and is strung with pretty white lights that twinkle in the evening hours.

DESSERT

Pinched into an adorable postage-stamp-sized green cottage, **◖ Mike's Ice Cream** (504 Oak St., 541/386-6260) scoops out luscious house-made cones and cups. In-season huckleberry shakes are enough to make you moan and the chocolate-chunked Galaxy really is out of this world. Enjoy it in the yard next to the cottage or scurry across the street to the hillside library lawn to watch downtown passersby and get some peek-a-boo glimpses of the Gorge.

MARKETS

If you're planning on picking up treats along the Fruit Loop drive, wait to completely stock up before you've had a chance to try some samples at **Packer Orchards and Bakery** (3900 SR 35, 541/234-4481, http://packerorchardsandbakery.com, 10 A.M.–6 P.M. daily). There are no gimmicky sights here, just the best darned jams, fruit butters, and pastries in the entire valley. Outside the shop you'll also be able to pick from bins overflowing with a wide selection of fresh fruits and veggies.

Don't just stop at the **Gorge White House** for the wine—a little out-building beside the house also delights with a unique smattering of fruits and prettily bottled house-made sauces. The coffee-merlot chocolate sauce tastes great with those apples you picked up on the Fruit Loop and the pear walnut sauce tosses well in any fruit or spinach salad.

You don't have to drive the Fruit Loop to tap into the fresh produce of the Hood River Valley. Pick up a bushelful of organic veggies or fruit at **Mother's Market Place** right in town. This small but bountiful market also runs a deli jammed with healthy and tasty options, many of which are vegan or gluten-free.

Information and Services

Hood River's go-to source of travel and tour information can be found at the city's main **visitor center** (20 E Port Marina Dr., 541/386-2000 or 800/366-3530, www.hoodriver.org, 9 A.M.–5 P.M. Mon–Fri. year-round, also 10 A.M.–5 P.M. Sat. May–Oct.) near the marina.

Transportation Network of The Dalles and **Columbia Area Transit** (http://community.gorge.net/hrctd) offer a fixed-route bus service between Hood River and Portland that runs every Thursday ($8 one-way), heading westbound in the morning and eastbound in the afternoon. The same service provider also runs a fixed-route service Monday through Friday between The Dalles and Hood River ($3 one-way). Buses arrive at and leave from the CAT station (224 Wasco Loop). Greyhound (www .greyhound.com) also offers bus service from this location, but you can't buy tickets at the station here.

THE DALLES AND VICINITY

East of Hood River, the Gorge takes a turn toward decidedly drier weather, with pine trees transitioning into grassy, sunny hillsides. Fortunately, this section of the south Gorge is home to some of the best riverside state parks and oxbow lakes in which adventuresome boaters, swimmers, and boarders can cool off in the water. At the eastern end of this stretch of I-84, The Dalles is a working class town that sports the largest population in the Gorge. Home to the fantastic Columbia Gorge Discovery Center and linked to Washington by The Dalles Dam and a peach-colored trussed bridge, the city presents a convenient spot to rest or take in a no-frills bite before making a U-turn north or south on a bi-state Gorge loop

drive. In between "the Hood" and The Dalles, the tiny town of Mosier is worth a mosey if you've got the time for delicious ice cream and a bike-ride through some 90-year-old tunnels blasted for the first Gorge highway.

Sights and Recreation
MOSIER TWIN TUNNELS

Explore one of the most popular abandoned stretches of the Historic Columbia River Highway from Mosier. Rehabilitated for walking and cycling, the paved **Twin Tunnels** trail runs five miles and passes through two tunnels that dig straight through the craggy basalt so familiar in this region. Stop in the tunnel to look through the cutaways to views of the Gorge, and check out the inside of the rock walls to see if you can spot the places where some travelers in 1921 carved their names while trapped there during a snowstorm.

MEMALOOSE STATE PARK

Situated directly in the hottest part of the Gorge, Memaloose State Park's 100-degree summer days can easily be relieved under the

A classic car crosses into The Dalles in style.

© ERICKA CHICKOWSKI

pretty maples and willows that shade and decorate this riverfront park. Windsurfers and kiteboarders can further cool off in the river from the popular launch point here, which provides views out to the island that gives the park its name. This was a sacred island to the Chinook Indian tribes of the Gorge, who used to lay their dead on open pyres there.

MAYER STATE PARK
Another favorite sunny-side destination in the Gorge, Mayer State Park holds within it some stunning views and a popular lake for fishing and swimming. First the view: the park covers a dramatic hillside overlooking the Gorge called Rowena Crest, which is summited by the twisting, turning segment of the Historic Columbia River Highway that runs through the park. It can also be hiked by trail. On the river itself, Mayer presents a place to launch windsurfing and kiteboarding equipment, plus a boat ramp.

COLUMBIA GORGE DISCOVERY CENTER
The pre-eminent museum in all of the Gorge makes its home in the unassuming town of The Dalles. The Columbia Gorge Discovery Center lays out a fascinating mix of exhibits detailing the geography, flora, fauna, history, and culture of the region. With presentations on the Lewis and Clark expedition, the building of the historic highway, and even an up-close-and-personal birds of prey demonstration, this museum makes the drive to The Dalles well worth it even if that's the only thing you do on the eastern section of the Gorge.

THE DALLES DAM
"The Dalles" is from the French (*La Grand Dalle de la Columbia,* meaning flagstone), a reference to the basaltic rocks lining the narrows. In the pre-dam days, this was the most dangerous point in the river for early navigators who approached a virtual staircase of rapids called Celilo Falls. Most Oregon Trail travelers opted to portage around the rapids at The Dalles. For centuries the falls were a major fishing spot for Native Americans who caught salmon as they

headed upstream to spawn. When Lewis and Clark visited this area in 1805, they reported a village of 21 large wooden houses and called the place a "great emporium . . .where all the neighboring nations assemble."

The Dalles Dam (exit 87 off of I-84, 541/506-7819) was completed in 1957 and the half-mile-long powerhouse now produces some 1.8 million kilowatts of power. Some salmon still make it up this far, and Native American fishing platforms can occasionally be found on both sides of the river. Check out the dam with a free tour through the power generation and fish passage areas. Tours leave the dam's visitor center at 11 A.M. and 2 P.M. on weekends between Memorial Day and Labor Day. Visitors have to be U.S. citizens, over 16 years old and must come with photo ID.

FORT DALLES
The Dalles initially sprang up as a pioneer and military outpost in the 19th century. Learn about the area's history, check out pioneer and military artifacts, and an interesting collection of antique wagons at **Fort Dalles Museum and Anderson Homestead** (500 W. 15th St, 541/296-4547, 10 A.M.–4 P.M. daily, $5). The museum is inside the old Surgeon's Quarters, the only remaining building left of the fort. Nearby, the Anderson Homestead is a quaint little cottage built of hand-hewn logs in 1895 and now furnished with antiques representative of the era.

DESCHUTES RIVER RAFTING
Splash your way up and over the Deschutes River east of The Dalles on a half-day, full-day, or overnight expedition led by **All Adventures Rafting** (509/493-3926, www.alladventures rafting.com, $79 for full-day trip). This long-time river-running outfit has been guiding these waters for over 40 years and can arrange exciting class III through class IV trips or set something up calmer for a raft and fish combination trip. Unlike many of the Columbia tributary whitewater trips that take you through frigid waters that require many layers of neoprene, this hot-weather trip is a tank-top and

sandals type run the way that most people envision rafting should be.

Entertainment and Events

Check out the gorgeous 1900s-era backbar at the historic **Baldwin Saloon** (205 Court St., 541/296-5666). Serving some of the finest wines the Gorge has to offer, the saloon is a might bit less rough and tumble than back when it was built in 1876 right near the town's train tracks. A squat brick building that's been restored with care, it is now highlighted by an 18-foot mahogany backbar with big scrolled columns and an original mirror trimmed with stained glass paneling.

Held the second weekend in July, the **Fort Dalles Days and Rodeo** (http://fortdalles days.com) is the big shindig in town each year. Expect to see the buckin' broncs of a pro rodeo, plus a street fair and 5K fun run.

Accommodations

Hidden away on a Gorge-view property featuring a colorful garden, a creek, and a little pond, **The Mosier House** (704 Third Ave., 541/478-3640 or 877/328-0351, www.mosierhouse .com, $85–145) lies in a beautiful Queen Anne Victorian built by the little town's founder in 1904. Each of the five rooms has its own unique benefits—one with pretty stained glass windows, another with a beautiful Gorge vista, another with a garden view, and so on.

The only hotel settled directly in the middle of The Dalles' historic district, **The Dalles Inn** (112 W. 2nd St., 888/935-2378) presents an affordably posh alternative. With sleek linens, pillow-top beds, flat screen televisions, and free Wi-Fi, rooms come with all the goodies. Also included are in-room coffee makers, fridges, and microwaves. The property sports a heated pool and fitness center and is extremely pet-friendly.

Even though the building's designed to look like a quaint farm building, **Cousins Country Inn** (2114 W. 6th St., 541/298-5161) won't make you feel like you're staying in a barn. The neutral palette and clean lines of the guest rooms feel more like a trendy urban inn.

Flat screen TVs, free Wi-Fi, and leather seats are the norm and some rooms come with fireplaces. The pool here is small, but there's a nice indoor whirlpool and you'll be able to work out for free at an offsite fitness center.

A boutiquey twist on the typical roadside stopover, **Celilo Inn** (3550 E. 2nd St., 541/769-0001) has sweeping views of the Gorge. Accented with chocolate-colored backboards and wine-colored chairs and throw pillows, the classy rooms appeal to the winetaster crowd who come here after a day tasting at Maryhill across the river. Enjoy a glass of wine on the patio or take a dip in the pool, both of which face the Columbia.

Food

Sharing a spic-and-span showroom garage with mint-condition vintage Porches in the tiny village of Mosier, **Route 30 Classics & Roadside Refreshments** serves delicious ice cream—huckleberry cheesecake is my favorite—and cold drinks. It makes a perfect stop after taking a ride through the nearby Twin Tunnels.

Overlooking the Gorge with a view of The Dalles Bridge, **The Bistro at Waters Edge** (541/506-5777, 6 A.M.–9 P.M. Mon.–Fri., 7 A.M.–8 P.M. Sat., 11 A.M.–6 P.M. Sun.) is run out of an airy space with plenty of windows. Serving a unique selection of sweet and savory crepes, plus flatbread pizza and typical café sandwich and salad fare, the Bistro presents a healthful alternative to many of the diner and drive-through options just off The Dalles's I-84 off-ramps. The patio's view is nice, but hold onto the napkins because its prime vantage point also lies right in the Gorge's blustery wind currents.

If it is a big, juicy burger that you crave, though, keep driving to **Big Jim's Drive-In** (2938 E. 2nd St., 541/298-5051, 10 A.M.–10 P.M. daily), a Gorge institution that's been running its fryers for over 40 years. If you're in a non-traditional fried spuds mood, give the joint's yummy Tater Tots a go and don't forget to pair your meal with a thick shake.

Serving up south-of-the-border specials, **La Fogata** (1204 Yakima Valley Hwy.,

509/839-9019, 11 A.M.–9 P.M. daily) is a simple taqueria that whips up a mean street taco. Pick from everything from standard carne asada to succulent beef cheek to fish, and slather on the freshly made salsa to complete the fiesta in your mouth. With only a couple of tables inside and a few picnic tables set up outside, this popular place can get crowded at times, but the wait is worth it.

Gussied up in a barn-red building with a shiny green tractor plopped down right in the middle of the dining room, **Cousins Restaurant and Lounge** plays up its country theme to the last, serving big portions of farm-style dishes like pot roast and meatloaf, accompanied by drinks served in Mason jars.

On the other end of the sophistication spectrum, **La Petite Provence** (408 E. 2nd St.), is a boulangerie and patisserie with deliciously fragrant French onion soup, crusty baguettes, and delectable sandwiches. A meal here is left unfinished without a sweet ending—the tortes, cookies, and sweet pastries can't be missed.

For a change of pace, you can switch your French accent to an Italian one and swing by **Romul's** (312 Court St., 541/296-9771, www .romuls.com) right down the street. A casual café with all the standard faves—calamari, lasagna, ossobuco—it does also surprise with a few dishes. Some delicious departures include stuffed grape leaves, pork schnitzel, and roasted duck cappelini.

Information and Services

You can gather information on local lodging, recreation and events at **The Dalles Chamber of Commerce** (404 W. 2nd St., 541/296-2231, www.thedalleschamber.com, 10 A.M.–5 P.M. Mon.–Fri.). **The Transportation Network of The Dalles** and **Columbia Area Transit** (http://community.gorge.net/hrctd) offer a fixed-route bus service between The Dalles and Portland that runs every Thursday ($8 one-way), heading westbound in the morning and eastbound in the afternoon. The same service provider also runs a fixed-route service Monday through Friday between The Dalles and Hood River ($3 one-way). Buses arrive at and leave from **The Dalles Transportation Center** (201 Federal St.). Greyhound (www .greyhound.com) also offers bus service from this location.

Yakima Valley

Yakima (YAK-a-ma) has become one of the largest cities in Central Washington and the commercial hub for the Yakima Valley. Eastern settlement was strongly resisted by the confederated tribes and bands of the Yakama Nation in the early 1800s. With the end of the 1855 Indian War and the settling of the Yakama People on a reservation, ranchers and farmers took their place, raising apples, pears, hops, and mint in large amounts. The volcanic soil practically farms itself. Today, Yakima relies on those crops still, as well as huge fields of hops for beer brewing. Yakima is also the source for the vast majority of grapes shipped all over the state to fuel the passion of boutique vintners. The extensive manpower needs of agriculture have brought a small army of men and women of Mexican extraction to the area. Thus, the valley has developed a rich culture of top-notch Mexican restaurants and upbeat music, far away from the border. Here, I-82 cuts across the north side of the valley, with the older Highway 22 following a parallel route on the south side. Several small towns dot the route between Yakima and the Tri-Cities; the largest are Zillah, Granger, Sunnyside, Grandview, and Prosser.

SIGHTS
Historic Yakima

The North Front Street Historical District boasts some of Yakima's oldest buildings, including the 1898 Lund Building and the Northern Pacific Railroad depot.

Three miles northwest of Yakima on

© ERICKA CHICKOWSKI

Wander the streets of Toppenish to see the city's murals.

Highway 12 you'll find the mysterious **Indian Painted Rocks,** a state historical site. Although the pictographs were partially destroyed by an early irrigation flume, some remain at Naches Highway and Powerhouse Road. The cliffs nearby are popular with local rock climbers.

The **Ahtanum Mission** (17740 Ahtanum Rd., 509/966-0865), east of Yakima along Ahtanum Creek, was built in 1852 by Catholic priests. During the Yakama Wars of the 1850s, the relationship between the priests and Yakamas led U.S. Army soldiers to the unlikely conclusion that the missionaries were providing the Yakama warriors with arms and munitions. A group of soldiers thus torched the mission in the middle of the night. The church was rebuilt in 1869 and is still used today. You can visit the mission and surrounding park for a small fee.

Toppenish Murals

Toppenish boasts that its chief recreation is watching paint dry. The city of murals and false-front Western buildings is a draw for lovers of outdoor art. Topics are generally of the sagebrush, saddles, and steam train variety.

Visit the chamber of commerce (11 S. Toppenish Ave., 509/865-3262, www.toppen ish.net, 10 A.M.–4 P.M. Mon.–Sat. Apr.–Oct.) to pick up a map of the 80-plus wall-art pieces, or hop aboard one of the wagon rides offered by **Toppenish Mural Tours** (509/697-8995, $12 adults, $5 kids, 10 A.M.–1 P.M. Mon.–Sat.) that leave from the depot area on one-hour tours May–September.

Museums

Start your visit to Yakima at the large **Yakima Valley Museum** (2105 Tieton Dr., Yakima, 509/248-0747, www.yakimavalleymuseum.org, 10 A.M.–5 P.M. Mon.–Sat. and 11 A.M.–5 P.M. Sun., $5 adults, $3 students and seniors, $12 families, free for under age 5). It boasts an extraordinary collection of Yakama Native American artifacts, Oregon Trail, and local fruit tree industry exhibits. Boxcars, shops, and tool sheds are arrayed around the property and available for self-guided touring.

YAKAMA RESERVATION

Toppenish is the capital of the Yakama Indian Nation and the commercial center for the 1.37-million-acre Yakama Reservation (509/865-5121). The tribal council decided in 1994 that the correct spelling for their tribe is Yakama, rather than Yakima, although it is formally known as the Confederated Tribes and Bands of the Yakama Nation. The reservation is home to approximately 5,000 Native people from 14 different tribes and bands, along with another 20,000 non-Indians. The Yakamas run several businesses including a furniture factory, a juice bottler, orchards, ranches, a casino, and a sawmill. The westernmost edge of the reservation includes land within the Mount Adams Wilderness, and a permit is required for camping, fishing, or hunting.

The **American Hop Museum** (22 S. B St., Toppenish, 509/865-4677, www.american hopmuseum.org, 10 A.M.–4 P.M. Wed.–Sat., 11 A.M.–4 P.M. Sun. May–Sept., closed Mon.–Tues., $3 adults, $2 students, free for children under 5) is the only one of its kind, shining a bright spotlight on the underappreciated hops, a vital bittering ingredient in the production of beer and ale and a huge local cash-crop.

The once-bustling 1911 railroad depot near Toppenish town square is home to a shrine to a force that made most of the northern half of Washington possible. No, not glaciers. The **Northern Pacific Railway Museum** (10 S. Asotin Ave., 509/865-1911, 10 A.M.–4 P.M. Tues.–Sat. and noon–4 P.M. Sun. May–Oct., $5). Explore rail and steam artifacts and a restored telegraph office.

The impressive **Yakama Cultural Heritage Center** (100 Spiel-yi Loop, 509/865-2800, www.yakamamuseum.com, 8 A.M.–5 P.M. daily, $5 adults, $3 seniors and children 11–18, $1 children under 10, $12 family of four, free for enrolled Yakama members) on the Yakama Reservation features a museum that tells the story of the Yakama Nation from its beginnings to the present, a library specializing in Native American books, a theater that presents first-run movies and stage productions, a restaurant, and an RV park.

Fort Simcoe State Park

Head 27 miles west from Toppenish through the heart of the Yakama Reservation to peaceful Fort Simcoe State Park (509/874-2372, www.parks.wa.gov, 6:30 A.M.–dusk daily April–Oct., free). The drive takes you through fields of grapes and hops, past fast-growing Heritage College, past Native American burial grounds with decorated gravesites, to the reconstructed remains of a U.S. Army fort built to guard the frontier in 1856.

Other Parks

More than 250 species of birds live in the marshy **Toppenish National Wildlife Refuge** (five mi. south on Hwy. 97, then south a half mile on Pump House Road, 509/865-2405). The interpretive center and nature trail will get you started.

The **Yakima Area Arboretum** (1401 Arboretum Drive, 509/248-7337, www.ahtrees.org, dawn–dusk daily) is a peaceful 46-acre park with a Japanese garden and bird sanctuary, plus over 2,000 specimens of native and exotic woody plants near I-90 and Nob Hill Boulevard.

Across the Yakima River from Union Gap, bird-watchers will want to visit the **Hazel Wolf Bird Sanctuary** at the Wenas Creek Campground in the Wenas Valley, five miles west of Selah on Wean Road. Over 100 species of birds have been sighted in the 40-acre sanctuary.

Wineries

Yakima Valley is one of the premier wine-growing regions in the entire state, covering two distinct viticultural appellations, Yakima Valley and Rattlesnake Hills. Stop at local visitors centers for a map of more than two dozen local wineries, or request a copy from the **Yakima**

Valley Wine Growers Association (800/258-7270, www.yakimavalleywine.com).

UPPER YAKIMA VALLEY

No need to truck deep into the valley for a charming vineyard experience. Keep close to the city and visit **The Tasting Room Yakima** (250 Ehler Rd., 509/966-0686) out near Cowiche Canyon. Here you'll encounter a small turn-of-the-20th-century farmhouse that acts as a cooperative tasting room to three boutique wineries. Outside, there is a verdant lawn and a patio, a well-tended garden, and a small chicken coop. All of this is adjacent to a small nine-acre biodynamic vineyard and over 80 more acres of sage land open to hiking.

RATTLESNAKE HILLS

The pleasantly fragrant vineyard grounds at **Bonair Winery** (500 S. Bonair Rd., Zillah, 509/829-6027, www.bonairwine.com, 10 A.M.–5 P.M. daily) also present great views of the mountain and of nearby orchards. Stop by the shady pond to give Bonair's resident Aussie shepherd dog a scritch behind the ears before heading into the new pale-yellow French chateau tasting room. You'll be greeted with a smile by the friendly owners, who have the gift of gab. Call ahead to arrange a guided vineyard or winery tour ($10).

Sit on a bench near a giant wine barrel to sip a glass and survey the surroundings at the **Hyatt Vineyards Winery** (2020 Gilbert Rd., Zillah, 509/829-6333, www.hyattvineyards .com, 11 A.M.–5 P.M. daily April–Oct., 11 A.M.–4:30 P.M. daily Nov.–Dec. and Feb.–Mar., closed Jan.). An immaculate lawn, colorful rose garden, and a giant windmill sit directly outside the tasting room patio. Surrounding them are acres of orderly vineyard rows.

The McDonald Mercantile building houses **Piety Flats Winery** (2560 Donald-Wapato

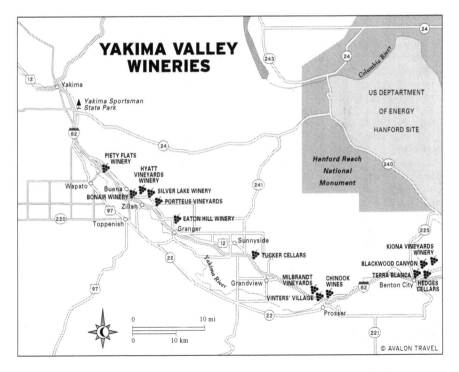

© ERICKA CHICKOWSKI

Walk the vineyards in the Yakima Valley for a closer look at the growing grapes.

Rd., 509/877-3115, 11 A.M.–5 P.M. Fri.–Sun., closed Dec.–Feb.). Surrounded by a lawn and table shaded by young walnut trees, this 1911 country store building offers bric-a-brac, candies, and gourmet foods to go along with the wine tastings.

The mezzanine tasting room at **Silver Lake Winery** (1500 Vintage Rd., Zillah, 509/829-6235, www.silverlakewinery.com, 11 A.M.–4 P.M. Thurs.–Mon. Dec.–Mar., 10 A.M.–5 P.M. daily Apr.–Nov.) affords a nice vineyard view and windows into the winery's distilling operation. The patio and porch are especially pretty in the fall when the leaves begin to turn.

You'll wind through gravel roads hugged by grapevines to get to the barrel room tasting bar at **Portteus Vineyards** (5201 Highland Dr., Zillah, 509/829-6970, www.portteus.com, noon–5 P.M. daily in summer, call for winter hours). Don't let the warehouselike atmosphere scare you away—the winemakers here produce some prized reds.

LOWER VALLEY AND PROSSER

Once a part of a vast fruit and vegetable

empire, the cannery building that holds **Eaton Hill Winery** (530 Gurley Rd., Granger, 509/854-2220, www.eatonhillwinery.com, 10 A.M.–5 P.M. daily) dates back to the early 1900s. See for yourself how barrels have replaced cans in this historic structure while you take a sip or two of the winery's award-winning gewürztraminer.

Tucker Cellars (70 Ray Rd., Sunnyside, 509/837-8701, www.tuckercellars.net) throws open the doors to its 10,000-square-foot facility and 50-acre vineyards for tours every day (10 A.M.–5 P.M. in summer, 10 A.M.–4 P.M. in winter). Once you've worked up an appetite, head to the on-site market to pick up a host of gourmet food grown, cooked, or canned by the Tucker family. Favorite treats include fresh fruit and produce, pickled asparagus spears, and home-popped white cloud corn.

Hugged by its own small vineyard and a stand of plum and cherry trees, the boutique **Chinook Wines** (220 Wittkopf Ln. off of Wine Country Rd., Prosser, 509/786-2725, www.chinookwines.com, noon–5 P.M. Sat.–Sun.) lies inside renovated farm buildings. Get a peek inside the winery and the barrel room before

ICE WINE

While a disaster for many, for some Washington vintners, crystalline frost over ripe grape clusters is a beautiful sight. In these parts, such a picture portends the prospect of ice wine, an intensely flavorful and sweet concoction that can only be produced when the stars align just so to give wineries the chance to create it.

Ice wine is pressed from grapes that have frozen while still on the vine. In order to make this happen, vineyards must take a gamble. They'll reserve a selection of grapes past harvest time, protecting them with nets from hungry birds and other critters, and hope that the frost falls before the grapes go bad. If the weather doesn't cooperate, the vine's precious cargo is lost.

If it does, the grapes must be picked immediately so they can be squeezed while still frozen. When a grape freezes on the vine, it's only the water in the fruit that seizes up. The sugars and solids in the grape remain unfrozen. So when it is pressed, that fruit yields only a fraction of the liquid a normal grape would, but it is a highly concentrated juice.

Ice wine is prized not only for its smoothness and flavor, but also for its rarity. Because it is produced so infrequently and because the grapes yield much less ice wine than normal wine, expect to pay a premium. But if you have the means, do give it a try. It is the smoothest dessert wine you'll ever sip.

Vintner's Village complex, a hub of 12 distinct wineries, and **The Winemaker's Loft** (357 Port St., 509/786-2705, 11 A.M.–6 P.M. daily), a new winery "incubator" that helps up-start winemakers experiment and launch their own brands. Some of the highlights among the Vintner's Village dozen include **Milbrandt Vineyards** (508 Cabernet Ct., 509/788-0030), which serves a varied tapas and salad menu to go with its vintages, and **Thurston Wolfe Winery** (588 Cabernet Ct., 509/945-4292, 11 A.M.–5 P.M. Thurs.–Sun.), known best for its full-bodied zinfandel, syrah, and sangiovese.

Also at the village is the funky **Airfield Estates** (560 Merlot Dr., 509/786-7401, www.airfieldwines.com, 11 A.M.–5 P.M. Sun.–Thurs., 10 A.M.–5 P.M. Fri.–Sat.), a lively winery whose decor plays off of its vineyard history—the vines were all planted around an old World War II airbase. The winery was built to resemble an old military hangar, including a 40-foot water tower that acts as a VIP tasting room and wine library for the facilities. Big band music pipes inside when you step into the gorgeous building and get a look through the giant picture windows that frame the barrel room. Airfield is open one hour later on summer Saturdays.

While you're in town, be sure to also drop in on **Desert Wind Winery** (2258 Wine Country Rd., Prosser, 509/786-7277), a handsome new winery that eschews the typical chateau motif. The buildings are made up like an old New Mexico adobe hut, with eclectic Southwest decor to match within the luxury tasting room. The property is also home to a four-room bed-and-breakfast and a sumptuous fine-dining establishment.

Benton City

The quiet small town of Benton City provides a sharp contrast to the bustling Tri-Cities, just a few miles to the east. Stop here to enjoy the lush valley with vineyards and fruit trees.

Melt into the comfy leather chairs inside the tasting room at **Kiona Vineyards Winery** (44612 N. Sunset NE, Benton City,

heading into the farmhouse tasting room. The personable owners happily welcome people to wander the grounds and spread out blankets and baskets in the shady garden picnic area. Be sure to bring some food that will pair well with the specialty sauvignon blanc.

The town of Prosser is a good place to survey the Yakima Valley wine scene without having to drive all over the countryside. In addition to the tasting rooms and wine bars scattered over town, Prosser is also home to the unique

509/588-6716, noon–5 P.M. daily). Step outside on the patio and lawn for a nice view of Red Mountain.

The facilities at **Blackwood Canyon** (53258 N. Sunset Rd., 509/588-7124, www.black woodwine.com, 10 A.M.–6 P.M. daily, $10 standard, $25 reserve) are nothing to get excited about, but that would detract from the wine anyway. The winery sits at the end of a rough gravel road in the middle of the vineyards, and the tasting room is just a counter in the warehouse. The real star of the show is the eccentric winemaker, a believer in old-method, small-batch fermentation processes that produce, hands down, the best wines in Yakima valley. If you have the time, he'll take you through several hours of tasting, even bringing out bits of food he's prepared to pair with his masterpieces. The chardonnays, cabernets, and late-harvest wines are quite distinctive.

Tour through the cool, dark wine-storage caves at **Terra Blanca** (34715 N. DeMoss Rd., Benton City, 509/588-6082, www.terrablanca .com, 11 A.M.–6 P.M. daily) on Red Mountain. The $15 tour (noon and 3 P.M. Sat.–Sun.) allows you to walk the caves, the fermentation bays, the barrel room, and the vineyard, followed up with a chance to taste the fruit of all the labor.

ENTERTAINMENT AND EVENTS
Performing Arts
The **Yakima Valley Community Band** (www .yakimacommunityband.org) has free concerts on Wednesdays and Thursdays throughout the summer, as well as a spring program. Summer concerts are held in one of several parks and create perfect opportunities for relaxing. The **Yakima Symphony Orchestra** (32 N. 3rd St., 509/248-1414, www.yakimasymphony .org) performs a diverse season of music at the Capitol Theater October–April.

A new hub of Yakima's performance community, **The Seasons Performance Hall** (101 N Naches Ave., 509/453-1888, www.theseasons yakima.com) has some of the best acoustics east of the Cascades. This grand old building was

converted from an old Seventh-day Adventist church and now draws quality jazz, classical, Latin, and world-beat musicians.

The historic **Capitol Theater** (19 S. 3rd St., 509/853-2787, www.capitoltheatre.org) is a beautifully restored 1920 theater, now hosting a full schedule of musical, theatrical, and Broadway productions.

Festivals and Events
The most popular local event is the **Central Washington State Fair** (1301 S. Fair Ave., 509/248-7160, www.fairfun.com) held in late September, which features a PRCA championship rodeo, hypnotists, carnival, nationally recognized musical talent, nitro-fueled demolition derby, and agricultural displays The **The Central Washington Antique Farm Expo** (509/457-8735) on the third weekend of August features an old-time threshing bee and working displays of farm equipment at the Central Washington Agricultural Museum.

The biggest annual wine event is the **Yakima Valley Spring Barrel Tasting** (800/251-0751) in late April, when the wineries pour samples of their new releases straight from the barrel and offer tours, hors d'oeuvres, and educational exhibits. All 25 wineries are open 10 A.M.–5 P.M. during this three-day event.

Dog lovers will enjoy Prosser's **National Championship Chukar Field Trials** on the last weekend in March. It attracts English pointers and shorthairs from all over the country.

Treaty Days and the All-Indian Rodeo and Pow Wow in nearby White Swan is held in early June to celebrate the signing of the Treaty of 1855. The rodeo features the Yakama Nation in a powwow and parade.

Fort Simcoe (509/874-2372) puts on a great show in June also, complete with living history presentations, traditional tribal dance, a flag-raising ceremony, military re-enactors, antique car shows, and best of all, free cake!

The 4th of July weekend brings a frenzy of activity to Toppenish: the **Pow Wow & Rodeo** (509/865-5566) is an event with something for everyone—a carnival, nightly rodeos, dancing, fireworks, a Wild West parade featuring cowboys, cowgirls, and Yakama people in full regalia, an antique power show, and arts and crafts booths.

The **Prosser Wine & Food Fair** (800/408-1517) on the second Saturday of August is the largest outdoor wine and food show in the state, attracting thousands of people for a chance to sample wine, beer, and food. The event usually sells out, so order advance tickets. It's only open to people over age 21.

In September, the Yakima Valley girds up to go ga-ga for the great **Grandview Grape Stomp** (114 Grandridge, 509/882-2100). In the town's grandest gala of the year, groups of three grapple to gouge grapes as in times gone by and gain some Grandview glory. And also a trophy. A fee of $30 gains you general admission and covers family activities galore.

The **Prosser Balloon Rally and Harvest Festival** (1230 Bennett Ave., www.prosser balloonrally.org) on the third weekend of September attracts balloon enthusiasts for morning launches and nighttime lighted balloons.

Late into the season, November brings **Tribal Jam** (509/865-5363, $25), a showplace for some of the country's best American Indian musicians and singers. The show is held at the Heritage Theater at the Cultural Heritage Center.

The season starts to wind down with **Thanksgiving in Yakima Valley Wine Country** (509/965-5201), which features food and wine-tasting at most local wineries. This is one way to taste a variety of gourmet foods and to get recipe ideas.

In early December, the **Country Christmas Lighted Farm Implement Parade** features bulb-bedecked tractors, farm machinery, and horse-drawn carriages and wagons in one of the premier lighted parades in the northwest. Call the Sunnyside Chamber of Commerce (509/837-5939) for details.

SHOPPING

At Yakima Avenue and North 1st, a trainful of 22 old railroad cars and pseudo-Victorian buildings house the **Track 29 Shopping Mall**

with gift shops and eateries. Several antique shops are inside the adjacent **Yesterday's Village.**

Several downtown art galleries offer high-quality works, including **Simon Edwards Gallery** (811 W. Yakima Ave., 509/453-7723).

Toppenish is rife with antique stores, craft shops, and gift shops. **The Amish Connection** (509/865-5300) has handcrafted Amish furniture, dolls, quilts, and other items. A few doors away is **Kraff's** (509/865-3000), the largest retailer of Pendleton blankets in the United States. **Roses Native Designs** (202 S. Toppenish Ave., 509/865-9325) offers local Native American art and crafts. For authentic Native American arts and crafts, visit the gift shop at **Yakama Nation Cultural Heritage Center.**

SPORTS AND RECREATION
Racing
The **Yakima Speedway** (1600 Pacific Ave., 509/248-0647, www.yakimaspeedway.us) hosts auto racing every Saturday night April–early October, ranging from Super Stocks to Youth Hornets. If that doesn't completely get your motor running, take part in the annual **Vintiques Northwest Nationals** (www.vintiques.com) car show and Rod Run held in late July and early August. You're bound to see some of the Northwest's finest mechanical muscle right here, plus a parts-oriented swapmeet, drag racing events, food, camping, and a carnival atmosphere.

Spectator Sports
Yakima County Stadium (1220 Pacific Ave., 509/452-1450) is home to the **Yakima Bears** (509/457-5151, www.yakimabears.com), a short-season class-A affiliate of the Arizona Diamondbacks. Games are affordable and the team offers several promotions throughout the June–September schedule.

Scenic Drives
Driving on I-82 between Ellensburg and Yakima, you'll realize that Central Washington

isn't the flat, boring terrain you might have heard about. As the road snakes up treeless ridges over 2,000 feet high, the far-off brown hills look as if they're covered with soft velvet; up close, it resolves into sagebrush, scrub, and grass. Pull into the rest stop at the south end of the Fred Rodmon Memorial bridge for a stunner of a view of the icy summits of Mount Adams and Mount Rainier in the distance.

The **Jacob Durr Wagon Road** (aka Wenas Road) is not recommended for vehicles without four-wheel drive. It was once the only route linking Yakima and Ellensburg; today, it's surely the most scenic, climbing over Umtanum Ridge for a 360-degree view of the Cascades and Yakima Valley. Drive north from Selah on N. Wenas Avenue, which becomes Wenas Road, the old Durr Wagon Road. The more standard route northward (I-90) also offers excellent vistas from the **Manatash Ridge Viewpoint** into the lush Kittitas Valley, with the Wenatchee Mountains rising behind the town of Ellensburg.

Water Sports

Yakima's **Franklin Park** (21st Avenue and Tieton Drive), has a big pool with a slippery spiral water slide. The grassy hills at this park are also a local hot spot for sledding in the winter.

At **Eschbach Park** (4811 South Naches Rd., 509/574-2435, www.co.yakimacounty.us), five miles past the fish hatchery on the Old Naches Highway, rent a tube or kayak and take a lazy float down the Naches River. The day-use, 168-acre county park offers boating, swimming, picnicking, and play areas.

Many locals also float, water ski, or fish (trophy-sized rainbows for catch-and-release fishing only) in the beautiful 27-mile **Yakima River Canyon** (509/665-2100) between Ellensburg and Yakima owned by the private Nature Conservancy. The river is paralleled by State Highway 821, with several boat ramps and picnic sites along the route and is home to the greatest concentration of nesting raptors in the state.

Before you head out to swish your rod

around, pick up a few flies and nymphs from **Fairbanks Out Centers** (423 West Yakima Ave., Yakima, 509/457-3474), whose helpful staff can point you in the right direction if you know what you're doing or sign you up for one of their guided excursions if you don't.

Cycling

The Yakima Valley farming country makes for great back-roads cycling, with a multitude of possible loop trips. Get a map of local cycling routes from the visitors center. Unfortunately, there are absolutely no bicycle rental shops in the Yakima Valley, Tri-Cities, or Walla Walla Valley areas. Pick up a rental on the way. If you are headed over via I-90, stop off at **Cle Elum Bike and Board** (316 W. 1st St., 509/674-4567). Or try one of the numerous rental shops in the Gorge if you are coming in from parts south.

If you need some supplies or want to buy a new ride in Yakima, **Jake's Bike Shop** (507 W. Nob Hill Blvd., 509/469-9602) is a friendly local bike store that does right by its customers.

Golf

Yakima has quite a few public courses. The **Apple Tree Resort** (8804 Occidental, 509/966-5877, www.appletreeresort.com, $50 nonresidents) features a signature par 3 17th hole—a tricky forced carry on to an apple-shaped island. **Suntides** (231 Pence Rd., 509/966-9065, $25) offers a par-70 course. The city-owned, executive-length **Fisher Park Golf Course** (823 S. 40th Ave., 509/575-6075) can be a nice, quick indulgence at $9.25 for nine holes. You can even rent clubs here. The **Westwood West Golf Course** (6408 Tieton Dr., 509/966-0890) is another executive course with a driving range. Nine holes will run you $28.

Hiking

The **Yakima River Greenway** encompasses 3,600 acres east of the city, connecting Selah, Yakima, and Union Gap along a 10-mile paved biking and walking path.

Cowiche Canyon is a scenic and remote

rocky canyon just a few minutes west of Naches. The abandoned railroad line ribbons along and across Cowiche Creek, passing distinctive rock formations, with some that resemble the Easter Island faces. The canyon is managed by Cowiche Canyon Conservancy (509/966-8608, www.cowichecanyon.org), which produces a brochure on the three-mile trail. To continue your journey, follow the out-and-back Uplands Trail spur off of the main trail. You can follow that about 1.5 miles to a shady grove of birch trees before returning.

ACCOMMODATIONS

Most of Yakima's in-town motels can be found along the Highway 97 corridor through town (1st Street).

Under $100

Cruise into town on Highway 82, cross the Yakima River, and take 1st to find the **Days Inn** (1504 N. 1st St., 509/248-3393 or 800/248-3360, $70 s or $75 d). Also affordable (and pet-friendly) is **Howard Johnson Plaza** (9 N. 9th St., 509/452-6511, $75 s or $95 d).

For valley accommodations, **Best Western Lincoln Inn** (515 S. Elm St., Toppenish, 509/865-7444 or 800/222-3161, www.bestwestern.com, $80s or $90 d) is the best choice in Toppenish, with its indoor pool, hot tub, exercise room, fridges, microwaves, and continental breakfast.

Farther east, **Sunnyside Inn B&B** (804 E. Edison, Sunnyside, 509/221-4195 or 800/221-4195, www.sunnysideinn.com, $89–99 d) is situated in the 1919 Fordyce house and has thirteen spacious rooms with private baths, eight of which feature whirlpool tubs. A hearty country breakfast is served, and kids are accepted.

Also in Sunnyside, **Country Inn and Suites** (408 Yakima Valley Hwy., Sunnyside, 509/837-7878 or 800/578-7878, $55 s or $66 d) has a heated outdoor pool, hot tub, and continental breakfast.

When you drive into Prosser, you can't miss **The Barn Motor Inn** (490 Wine Country Rd., 509/786-2121, $50 s or $55 d). Just like the name tells you, this motel is fashioned like a big red country barn. Rates are pretty good for the level of cleanliness and comfort offered by the rooms here. There's a pool and a restaurant on-site. You can also park RVs in the trailer facility around back ($17.50).

$100-150

Quality Inn Comfort Suites (I-82 and Valley Mall Blvd., 509/249-1900 or 800/228-5150, www.choicehotels.com, $129 s or $140 d) looks out over islands in the Yakima River. This all-suites motel has an indoor pool, hot tub, exercise room, continental breakfast, and free wireless Internet.

Holiday Inn Express (1001 E. A St., 509/249-1000 or 800/315-2621, www.hiexpress.com, $140 s or d) features an indoor pool, hot tub, fitness room, and continental breakfast. An extra $20 will warm the staff toward the idea of your pet staying the night with you.

A classic Queen Anne Victorian built in 1889, **A Touch of Europe B&B** (220 N. 16th Ave., 509/454-9775 or 888/438-7073, www.winesnw.com/toucheuropeb&b, $123–136 s or d) serves candlelit European breakfasts (included in rate), high tea ($30), and lavish five- to seven-course dinners ($50) in its elegant dining room. The German- and English-speaking owners provide an acre of shady grounds and three well-appointed guest rooms in a relaxing adults-only environment.

At the **Birchfield Manor B&B** (2018 Birchfield Rd., 509/452-1960 or 800/375-3420, www.birchfieldmanor.com, $119–220 d), guests may sample from a wine cellar amply stocked with local vintages. The biggest local B&B, Birchfield plumps the pillows for guests in four luxurious rooms in the 1910 main house and four adjacent, newer cottages. All rooms have private baths with whirlpool tubs, and some are equipped with gas fireplaces and private decks. The parklike grounds contain a swimming pool. Breakfasts are memorable, and dinners in the restaurant here are some of the finest around (Thurs.–Sat., $27–38 for full dinners). Ask about the golf packages in partnership with the Apple Tree Resort.

Orchard Inn B&B (1207 Pecks Canyon Dr., 509/966-1283, www.orchardinnbb.com, $109–129 d) is a lovely contemporary home tucked away in an orchard of cherry trees. The three guest rooms have private baths, private entrances, and the use of outdoor gazebos. A full, slow-food breakfast is served. The friendly bilingual (German and English) owners welcome kids and well-behaved dogs on approval.

$150-200

Feed a horse an apple grown right outside your door at **Cherry Wood Bed and Breakfast** (3271 Roza Dr., Zillah, 509/829-3500, www.cherrywoodbandb.com, $145–165 d), a fun little gem hidden away on a working farm in Zillah. This quirky inn offers a few different lodging options. First there are very comfortable and well-appointed rooms within the farmhouse, available year-round. Then there are the luxury teepee and themed retro trailers that open up in the warm summer months. Many guests stick around after breakfast for the host's guided horseback winery tours ($150), offered by appointment.

Over in Grandview, you'll be pampered from the get-go when you set your suitcases down at **Cozy Rose Inn B&B** (1220 Forsell Rd., 509/882-4669, www.cozyroseinn.com, $189 d). Lush tapestries, soft bedding, and smartly painted designer rooms await you here. All suites come with whirlpool tub and big-screen TV, and each has individual amenities including fireplaces, fridges, and private entrances. For maximum romance, breakfast can be delivered to your door and a special dinner can be arranged with the innkeeper.

Over $250

Dust off your fancy cowboy hat and tuck yourself in the luxurious rooms at the Southwest-style **Desert Wind Winery Inn** (2258 Wine Country Rd., Prosser, 509/786-7277, www.desertwindwinery.com, $250–300 d). The concert-hall-sized suites all come equipped with gas kiva fireplaces, large-screen TVs with Bose sound and DVD players, and balconies overlooking the winery courtyard and the Yakima River.

Camping

About a mile east of town off I-82, an oasis of green awaits at **Yakima Sportsman State Park.** Year-round, kids can fish the pond, stocked with bluegill, trout, catfish, and carp. Adults can try their luck on the nearby Yakima River. Tent sites run $21 and RV sites are $31. Americans with Disabilities Act (ADA)–compliant sites are available, as are coin-operated showers. Be sure to tackle the miles of hiking trails while you're here. Make reservations ($7 extra) at 888/226-7688, www.parks.wa.gov.

Wenas Creek Campground is home to the Hazel Wolf Bird Sanctuary in the Wenas Valley. Camping here is primitive—we mean it! There is no fresh water available and you can expect to dig your own trenches.

Trailer Inns (1610 N. 1st St., 509/452-9561 or 800/659-4784, www.trailerinnsrv.com, $22–40 depending on electricity needed) has a heated pool and a propane concession.

The **Yakama Nation Resort RV Park** (280 Buster Rd., 509/865-2000 or 800/874-3087, www.winesnw.com/YakNtnRVListing.htm), next to the Cultural Heritage Center has 125 parking spaces for RVs ($32), plus 14 very popular tepees ($30–50), a tent-camping area ($20), outdoor pool, hot tub, two saunas, exercise room, and other facilities.

FOOD
Yakima

One of the top 10 most-visited drive-ins in the country, **Miner's Drive-In** (2415 S. 1st St., 509/457-8194, 8:30 A.M.–4 A.M. daily) is a Yakima institution. The loyal customers line up for the flying-saucer-sized burgers and golden onion rings. Miner's also serves a book-length list of milk shake flavors. Freshness is the key here—you'll see the phrase "Nothing is cooked until you order it!" on signs in the store.

Looking for just the cure for a wine-induced hangover? Head to the local greasy spoon, **Mel's Diner** (314 N. 1st St., 509/248-5382, open 24 hours) and get yourself a big ol' breakfast with a fresh cup or three of coffee served up by waitresses who'll call you "hon."

Jack's Sports Bar (432 S. 48th Ave.,

Nosh on the best burgers in Yakima at Miner's Drive-In.

509/966-4340) is a fun place with burgers, sandwiches, and a big-screen TV, open till 1:45 A.M. on the weekends.

One of Yakima's finest supper spots, **Birchfield Manor** (2018 Birchfield Rd., two mi. east of the city on Birchfield Rd., 509/452-1960 or 800/375-3420, www.geopics.net/birchfield, dinner Thurs.–Sat.) seats diners in a restored 1910 farmhouse. Formal dinners are complemented by a vast selection of Yakima Valley wines. The innovative cuisine changes seasonally, but there is always a perfect filet mignon. Reservations are essential.

In the historic district, **The Greystone Restaurant** (5 N. Front St., 509/248-9801, entrées $30) aspires to be a fine dining establishment on par with big city cousins over in Seattle, and it certainly does have some strong points. The towering ceilings with antique molding and the ruggedly elegant exposed stonework certainly make for a dramatic dining room, and the food is delicious, even if the service is lacking. Your best bet is to bring some lively companions to pass the time, sit in the lounge, and order a bottle of wine with some scrumptious light appetizers.

Then head across the street to **The Depot Restaurant and Lounge** (32 N. Front St., 509/949-4233, 11:30 A.M.–10 P.M. daily, entrées $20), in Yakima's old 1910 Pacific Northern Railroad station, which has an equally exciting dining room and none of the pretense. The depot is beautifully restored, and you'll likely spend parts of dinner looking upward, mouth agape, at the molding and scrollwork in the domed ceiling. The chef dishes out mouthwatering plates of seafood, chops, and fresh salads at extremely reasonable prices.

Yakima far and away has the area's best Mexican restaurants, a gift from the many workers of Mexican descent that come here and make the region's agriculture such a success.

One of the best spots in town is at **Los Hernandez** (3706 Main St., Union Gap, 509/457-6003, 11 A.M.–6 P.M. Tues.–Fri., 10 A.M.–7 P.M. Sat., 11 A.M.–6 P.M. Sun., closed Mon.), which serves homemade tamales better than you'll get even in Southern California. You'll regularly see folks load up coolers full of them to take home. If you go in springtime, be on the lookout for the inventive asparagus tamales. They may sound strange, but they sure are delicious.

Santiago's Gourmet Restaurant (111 E. Yakima Ave., 509/453-1644, www.santiagos .org, 11:30 A.M.–2 P.M. and 5–9 P.M. Mon.–Fri., 5–10 P.M. Sat., closed Sun.) is a lively and popular Mexican restaurant with all the standards and excellent daily specials.

El Pastor (315 W. Walnut, 509/453-5159, 11 A.M.–8 P.M. Mon.–Fri., noon–8 P.M. Sat.) is a small place with inexpensive and delicious Mexican dishes. Find lots more *tortillerías* and *panaderías* on South 1st Street heading toward Union Gap.

For gourmet Italian food and Northwest specialties, visit **Gasparetti's** (1013 N. 1st St., 509/248-0628, http://gasperettisrestaurant. com, 11 A.M.–midnight daily). The pastas are all freshly made, and desserts are a real treat. Interestingly enough, it is also well known for its onion rings. You really can't do wrong giving them a try.

Let the chef win you over at **Keoki's Oriental Restaurant** (2107 W. Lincoln Ave., 509/453-2401, 11 A.M.–2 P.M. and 4–10 P.M. daily), where the cooking takes place at your table teppanyaki-style. The teriyaki steak is always a pleaser.

Finding food out in the winery back roads can be a hit-or-miss affair. Load up on picnic supplies in town before you head out to ensure a happy and fulfilling wine excursion. **Deep Sea Deli** (20 N. 9th Ave, 509/248-1484, 9 A.M.–6 P.M. Mon.–Sat., closed Sun.) stocks specialty cheese, meats, and crackers. It also smokes its own salmon right on the property. Or leave the lunch packing up to **Buhrmaster Baking Co. and Restaurant** (117 E 3rd Ave in Selah, 509/469-9973, www.buhrmaster bakingco.com, 8 A.M.–8 P.M. Mon.–Fri., 11 A.M.–8 P.M. Sat., closed Sun.), which prepares box lunches to go for wine tourists.

Fresh fruit, vegetable stands, and U-pick places can be found throughout the Yakima Valley. From Yakima, the easiest way to find them is to take Highway 97 and exit off Lateral A Road. Head down south and let the signs guide you. The farm roads are ruler-straight, so it is pretty much impossible to get lost.

One sure winner is **Barrett Orchards** (1209 Pecks Canyon Rd., 509/966-1275, www .treeripened.com), where you can pick cherries, pears, apples, peaches, or whatever is in season. Or let them do the work and buy from its farm store. It's also fun to just head down Highways 97 and 22 until something looks interesting— hand-painted signs are as numerous as the fruit they advertise.

Valley Eats

Toppenish's strong Mexican culture is evidenced in the town's restaurants, clothing stores, and songs on the radio. **Taqueria Mexicana** (105½ S. Alder St., 509/865-7116) has the best south-of-the-border meals in town.

Also near Toppenish, the **Yakama Nation Cultural Center** (100 Spiel-yi Loop, 509/865-2800) has a popular restaurant with a large salad bar, salmon, buffalo, and fry bread. The Sunday brunch is very popular.

You'll discover the best burgers around, along with floats, shakes, and cold drinks, at the old-fashioned soda fountain in **Gibbons Pharmacy** (117 S. Toppenish Ave., 509/865-2722).

Sunnyside's big Darigold cheese factory is one of the largest cheese plants in the nation. **Darigold Dairy Fair** (400 Alexander Rd., 509/837-4321, www.darigold.com) has self-guided tours, fun exhibits (including flying cows), and videos, plus fresh ice cream, cheeses, sandwiches, and gifts.

Snipes Mountain Brewing Inc. (905 Yakima Valley Hwy., Sunnyside, 509/837-2739, www.snipesmountain.com, 10 A.M.–10 P.M. Sun.–Fri., 11 A.M.–11 P.M. Sat.) is hard to miss. It's the huge log-and-lodgepole building near the center of town, with a brewery behind glass and a diverse menu that includes everything from wood-fired pizzas to seafood satay. It's very popular, with a lively atmosphere and tasty grub.

The Barn Inn and Restaurant (490 Wine Country Rd., 509/786-1131, www.thebarn motorinn.com) on the west end of Prosser is one of the best local restaurants for all-American steak and seafood platters; munch the great appetizers while watching sports on the big-screen TV. Another local favorite is **Picazo 717** (717 6th St., 509/987-1607, www.picazo717.com), an arty, modern tapas and wine bar that serves food that will make you want to sing. Try the daring shellfish cakes ($10) with shrimp, crab, and scallops drizzled with a poblano remoulade. Or bring a friend and order the paella for two ($34). The well-educated staff is ready to offer the perfect wine pairing from the jam-packed cellar.

The **Prosser Farmers Market** (509/786-9174, 8 A.M.–12:30 P.M. Sat. June–Sept.) takes place in the city park.

INFORMATION AND SERVICES

For maps, brochures, and current festival information, contact the **Yakima Valley Visitors and Convention Bureau** (10 N. 8th St., 509/575-3010 or 800/221-0751, www.visit yakima.com, 8 A.M.–5 P.M. Mon.–Fri. all year, plus 9 A.M.–5 P.M. Sat. and 10 A.M.–4 P.M. Sun. May–Oct.).

Emergency medical service is provided by **Yakima Valley Memorial Hospital** (2811 Tieton Dr., 509/575-8000) in the city. Emergency medical care is also available at the 63-bed **Toppenish Community Hospital** (502 West 4th Ave., 509/865-3105) which, along with high-tech care, also provides a Native American Spiritual Care Center featuring facilities for performing healing rituals and ceremonies. **Sunnyside Community Hospital** (10th & Tacoma, 509/837-1500) runs a 24-hour ER.

Sick pets are welcomed at **Pet Emergency Service** (510 W Chestnut Ave., 509/452-4138) in Yakima or at the **Wapato Toppenish Veterinary Clinic** (Hwy. 97 and Branch Rd., 509/865-3435).

GETTING THERE AND AROUND
By Air
The **Yakima Air Terminal-McAllister Field** (2300 West Washington Ave., 509/575-6149) is the largest airport in the area. **Alaska Airlines** (800/252-7522, www.alaskaair.com) provides daily passenger service to and from Sea-Tac Airport.

Several rental car agencies have desks here as well.

By Bus
Yakima Transit (509/575-6175, www.ci.yakima.wa.us/services/transit/) serves the Yakima area, including the municipal airport, with Monday–Saturday service.

For local tours, contact **Accent! Tours** (509/575-3949 or 800/735-0428, www.accenttours.com).

To get out of town or across the country, hop aboard **Greyhound** (509/457-5131 or 800/231-2222, www.greyhound.com) from its Yakima station (602 East Yakima Ave.). Greyhound also stops in Toppenish (at the Branding Iron, 509/865-3773) and Sunnyside (13th St. and Hwy. 12, 509/837-5344).

Tri-Cities

The sun-scorched confluence of the Snake and Columbia Rivers marks the end of a straight-shot journey along Highway 14 and the Columbia Gorge. Here you'll find an industrious trio of cities—Kennewick, Pasco, and Richland—at the rivers' junction. The Tri-Cities are book-ended by the Yakima and Walla Walla Valleys, surrounded by bountiful fields of potatoes, grains, fruits, and veggies, much of which is exported to Pacific Rim countries.

So how does a collection of agricultural towns grow into a metropolitan area with more than 120,000 people? The answer lies north of Richland at Hanford Site, birthplace of the Manhattan Project and home to the decommissioned nuclear munitions plant whose cleanup has funneled more than $12 billion into the local economy. Lucky visitors can get an up-close look at selected portions of Hanford site during limited tours offered by the Department of Energy.

SIGHTS
Hanford Site
In a cloak of secrecy that not even the workers who built it could see through, Hanford's Plant B reactor was the birthplace of the atomic age. This was the first large-scale plutonium production reactor ever to be built, creating a supply chain of radioactive materials that made it possible to create the first atomic bomb and Fat Man, the bomb that was dropped over Nagasaki, Japan, contributing to the end of World War II.

Since being decommissioned in 1968, Plant B has been meticulously scrubbed as a part of a decades-long, $1 billion-per-year cleanup of the entire Hanford Site nuclear complex. Though this historic reactor is still contaminated with radiation, visitors can't be harmed simply by coming into contact with objects there.

For several years now the Department of Energy has offered selected road tours around

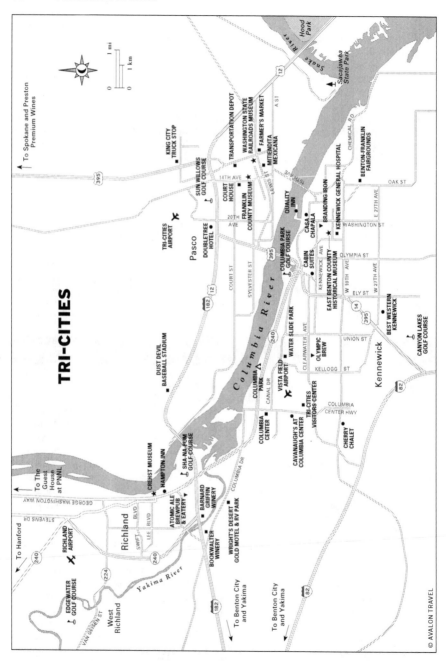

TRI-CITIES

Hood Park

Snake River

Sacajawea State Park

To Spokane and Preston Premium Wines

KING CITY TRUCK STOP

TRANSPORTATION DEPOT

WASHINGTON STATE RAILROADS MUSEUM

FARMER'S MARKET

MI TIENDITA MEXICANA

A ST

SUN WILLOWS GOLF COURSE

14TH AVE

COURT HOUSE

FRANKLIN COUNTY MUSEUM

QUALITY INN

KENNEWICK GENERAL HOSPITAL

BENTON-FRANKLIN FAIRGROUNDS

OAK ST

E 27TH AVE

CASA CHAPALA

BRANDING IRON

WASHINGTON ST

TRI-CITIES AIRPORT

DOUBLETREE HOTEL

Pasco

20TH AVE

SYLVESTER ST

COURT ST

Columbia River

COLUMBIA PARK GOLF COURSE

395

CABIN SUITES

KENNEWICK AVE

OLYMPIA ST

W 10TH AVE

W 27TH AVE

EAST BENTON COUNTY HISTORICAL MUSEUM

ELY ST

14

BEST WESTERN KENNEWICK

395

CANYON LAKES GOLF COURSE

DUST DEVIL BASEBALL STADIUM

182

12

240

WATER SLIDE PARK

CLEARWATER AVE

UNION ST

OLYMPIC BREW

KELLOGG ST

Kennewick

82

COLUMBIA PARK

VISTA FIELD AIRPORT

CANAL DR

COLUMBIA CENTER

TRI-CITIES VISITORS CENTER

COLUMBIA CENTER HWY

CAVANAUGH'S AT COLUMBIA CENTER

CHERRY CHALET

CREHST MUSEUM

HAMPTON INN

SHA-NA-PUM GOLF COURSE

To The Guest House at PNNL

GEORGE WASHINGTON WAY

BLVD

LEE BLVD

SWIFT

ATOMIC ALE BREWPUB & EATERY

BARNARD GRIFFIN WINERY

COLUMBIA DR

To Hanford

240

RICHLAND AIRPORT

Richland

STEVENS DR

BOOKWALTER WINERY

WRIGHT'S DESERT GOLD MOTEL & RV PARK

224

EDGEWATER GOLF COURSE

VAN GIESEN ST

West Richland

Yakima River

182

To Benton City and Yakima

82

To Benton City and Yakima

0   1 mi

0   1 km

© AVALON TRAVEL

limited areas of Hanford that include a walking tour of Plant B (www.hanford.gov/public tours). In order to book a slot, you must be an adult U.S. citizen who can plan well in advance. Online bookings fill up extremely quickly once the DoE announces the tour schedule. The only way to snag a free ticket is to regularly check the website. Plant B's availability may soon be opening up, though. In 2008 the building was placed on the National Registry of Historic Places, and DoE officials are currently working on plans to open the reactor to more public visits.

In spite of Hanford's toxic legacy, in a remarkable twist of fate it was also single-handedly responsible for preserving the last free-flowing, nontidal stretch of the "River of the West." The 51-square-mile buffer needed to protect outsiders from Hanford and vice versa during World War II and the Cold War is now protected as **Hanford Reach National Monument,** an amazing preserve that helps sustain healthy runs of chinook salmon and offers safe haven for deer, coyotes, bobcats, white pelicans, and other flora and fauna. For more information,

A NUCLEAR LEGACY

Cruise around the Tri-Cities and you'll find Atomic Ale Brewpub & Eatery, Atomic Body Shop, Atomic Laundry, Atomic Foods, and Atomic Health Center. The local high school team's name is the Bombers, with an atomic mushroom cloud as its emblem. There's a reason for this – the 560-square-mile Hanford Site just north of Richland, the source of much of the plutonium in America's nuclear arsenal.

During World War II, the United States began a frenzied race to develop an atomic bomb. The first controlled nuclear chain reaction experiments were conducted in late 1942, and within a few months the government had selected the Hanford site for its plutonium production plant. The location seemed perfect: remote enough for secrecy and safety, but still near railroads, an abundant source of water for cooling, and hydroelectric power for energy. The entire Manhattan Project was conducted with such secrecy that few of the construction workers knew what they were building. Three plutonium production reactors came online in time to provide the concentrated nuclear material for the bomb dropped on Nagasaki, Japan.

During the Cold War, the need for plutonium began to taper off, and the facility closed its doors, although the Hanford Site is still home to a Washington Public Power Supply System (WPPSS) nuclear plant.

After the closing of the last plutonium reactor, the environmental problems that had been shrouded in secrecy for more than 45 years began to surface. Left behind were 54 million gallons of radioactive waste and powdery radioactive iodine spread around the local flora. Quite a bit of waste was stored in leaky containers that had gradually drained into the groundwater.

In 1994, the U.S. Department of Energy, the Washington State Department of Ecology, and the U.S. Environmental Protection Agency began the full-scale cleanup. The easiest problems at Hanford have been resolved in the last few years, but real problems remain, particularly the toxic stew of radioactive waste that sits in underground tanks or has escaped into the ground.

One surprising effect of the shutdown of Hanford and subsequent cleanup has been that it has spawned economic growth in the Tri-Cities. Billions of dollars in federal funds have flowed into the region, providing employment for thousands of engineers, spill experts, construction workers, and others. With an eventual price tag of somewhere between $30 billion and $100 billion, the environmental cleanup has proven to be a far bigger project than the reactors ever were. Due to the need for professionals to perform local research, the little town of Kennewick has managed to attract a higher concentration of PhDs per capita than in any other town in the western United States.

contact the U.S. Fish and Wildlife Service Monument/Refuge headquarters at 509/371-1801 or www.hanford.gov/doe/culres.

Museums

The **Columbia River Exhibition of History, Science, and Technology** (95 Lee Blvd., Richland, 509/943-9000, www.crehst.org, 10 A.M.–5 P.M. Mon.–Sat., noon–5 P.M. Sun., $4 adults, $3 seniors, $2.50 children) best illustrates the Tri-Cities' split personality with agricultural and natural displays on one side, and nuclear exhibits on the other. Try out a "hot cell" manipulator arm or learn to name all the local Columbia fish species on sight.

The **Washington State Railroads Historical Society Museum** (122 N. Tacoma Ave., 509/543-4159, www.wsrhs .org, noon–4 P.M. Thurs.–Fri., 9 A.M.–3 P.M. Sat., $2 adults, $1 senior and teen, free 12 and under) has railroad memorabilia inside and display of antique locomotives and railcars outside.

City Parks

Columbia Park (509/783-3711, www.ci .kennewick.wa.us, open year-round) forms a 609-acre border along the south shore of the Columbia River (Lake Wallula) in Kennewick, with four boat ramps for fishing and waterskiing, an 18-hole golf course, tennis courts, a picnic area, nature trails, and campsites ($7) and RV spaces ($11). One of the main attractions is a six-mile paved path that's a favorite of cyclists, in-line skaters, joggers, and lovers out for a riverside stroll. Two other popular spots are the **Columbia Park Family Fishing Pond** and **Playground of Dreams.** The pond was built by a consortium of community groups, and the playground was constructed in five days with help from over 5,000 volunteers.

Lake Sacajawea

Nine miles east of Pasco on the Snake River, **Ice Harbor Lock and Dam** is the first of four dams on the Lower Snake, with one of the highest single-lift locks in the world, rising 103 feet. Take a self-guided tour, watch the eager fish climb the ladders, or stop by the visitors center (9 A.M.–5 P.M. daily Apr.–Oct.).

The dam creates Lake Sacajawea, accessible for fishing, waterskiing, or swimming at **Levey Park** on the Pasco-Kahlotus Road on the lake's west side, and Charbonneau and Fishhook Parks on the east side. **Charbonneau Park** (14 mi. northeast of Pasco, 509/547-7783, Apr.–Oct., $18–22) and **Fishhook Park** (off Highway 124, May–mid-Sept., $14–22) have campsites with water, fire rings, and showers. Make reservations for both these Army Corps of Engineers campgrounds at 518/885-3639, 877/444-6777, or www.reserveusa.com.

Lake Wallula

Five miles east of Kennewick off Finley Road, **Two Rivers County Park** is open daily for boating, swimming, and picnicking along the Columbia River/Lake Wallula.

The U.S. Army Corps of Engineers operates **Hood Park** (four mi. southeast of Pasco, 877/444-6777, May–mid-Sept., $18–20), just east of Pasco for boating, swimming, and picnicking. You can also camp here, on the Snake River near its confluence with the Columbia. Make reservations at 518/885-3639, 877/444-6777, or www.reserveusa.com.

Sacajawea State Park

Two miles east of Pasco off Highway 12, Sacajawea State Park (509/545-2361, www .parks.wa.gov, 6:30 A.M.–dusk Wed.–Sun. Apr.–Sept.) sits at the confluence of the Snake and Columbia Rivers at the site where Lewis and Clark camped in 1805 on their way to the Pacific Ocean. You can fish, water-ski, or picnic here. An **interpretive center** (1–5 P.M. Fri.–Tues.) contains exhibits on Sacajawea— the Shoshone woman who acted as interpreter for the Lewis and Clark party—plus information about the expedition, videos, and Native American artifacts.

Juniper Dunes Wilderness

This 7,140-acre parcel of Bureau of Land

Management (BLM) wilderness (509/536-1200) is 16 miles northeast of Pasco on Pasco-Kahlotus Road. It contains the six largest remaining western juniper groves in Washington, along with sand dunes that top 120 feet high and are up to 1,200 feet long. Access is only through private land, so you'll need to get the permission of local ranchers to reach the dunes, and you may need a 4WD vehicle for the last several miles of road. There are no trails or drinking water, and summer temperatures often exceed 100°F, so come prepared. The best time to visit is in the spring and fall, when temperatures are more moderate.

Wineries

Most of the best wine-tasting around the Tri-Cities can be found to the east in the Yakima Valley and to the west in Walla Walla valley. However, travelers on a tight schedule can still find enough wineries close by to fill up a pleasant afternoon.

The parklike grounds at **Preston Premium Wines** (509/545-1990, www.prestonwines .com, 10 A.M.–5:30 P.M. daily) are perfect for a grassy reverie. The second-story deck off the tasting room overlooks the vineyards and a grassy area lined with birch trees and flower beds. Take a stroll and enjoy the antique tractors and shady gazebo. The tasting room sells a selection of gourmet goodies to get that picnic started on the right foot.

Ask the expert staff at **Bookwalter Winery** (894 Tulip Ln., Richland, 509/627-5000, www.bookwalterwines.com, 10 A.M.–8 P.M. Mon.–Tues., 10 A.M.–11 P.M. Wed.–Sat., 10 A.M.–6 P.M. Sun.) for help pairing tasting wines with the artisan cheeses and meats offered in its first-rate tasting room. Slide into a stool at the tasting bar or set up shop in the garden patio. In the evening hours you'll be serenaded by the live music acts that play here. If you go to Bookwalter, be sure to make time to also stop in at neighboring **Barnard Griffin Winery** (878 Tulip Lane, Richland, 509/627-0266, www.barnardgriffin.com, 10 A.M.–5 P.M. daily).

ENTERTAINMENT AND EVENTS
Nightlife

The **Louie's Lounge** (1101 N. Columbia Center Blvd., Kennewick, 509/783-0611) at Red Lion Columbia Center hosts lively karaoke nights on Friday, Saturday, and Sunday. **Branding Iron** (109 W. Kennewick Ave., 509/586-9292, www.brandingironnightclub .com, 4 P.M.–1:30 A.M. Wed.–Sat.) plays live country and other types of music and opens up its big dance floor Thursday–Saturday and hosts karaoke on Wednesday.

The Arts

For those of classical taste, enjoy events staged by the **Mid-Columbia Symphony** (1177 Jadwin Ave., Richland, 509/943-6602, www.mid columbiasymphony.org), which has been around for more than 50 years. The **Mid-Columbia Regional Ballet** (1405 Goethals, Richland, 509/946-1531, www.midcolumbiaballet.org) stages a spring program as well as the wintertime favorite, *The Nutcracker*. **Columbia Basin College Performing Arts** (509/547-0511) at Columbia Basin College offers live concerts, theater, gallery showings, and literary events.

Festivals and Events

The festival season kicks into high gear with the **Cinco de Mayo** parade and festivities in Pasco. The **Columbia Valley Wineries Barrel Tasting** in early June is a favorite introduction to local wineries.

Richland's **Sunfest** (509/736-0510) is a summer-long series of weekend activities that feature international food, music, and dancing. Sunfest events include the **Tri-Cities Children's Festival** in mid-June, **Ye Merrie Greenwood Renaissance Faire** in late June, and the **Sidewalk Art Show** in late July—southeast Washington's largest arts and crafts show.

The Tri-Cities' biggest event is the annual **Unlimited Hydroplane races** on the Columbia River, the highlight of the late-July **Columbia Cup** (509/547-2203, www.waterfollies.com). The action centers on Columbia Park in Kennewick, but you can also watch from the Pasco side if you don't mind the sun in your face. Get to the park early on Friday or Saturday to take a pit tour before the races. A talent show, parade, and military aerial demonstrations round out the **Tri-Cities Water Follies** week.

Kennewick hosts the **Benton Franklin Fair and Rodeo** (1500 S. Oak St., 509/586-9211, http://bentonfranklinfair.com) every August, with top entertainers performing at the fairgrounds, including the Atomic City Rollergirls—if you're lucky. November brings the **Tri-Cities Wine Festival** (509/736-0510, www.tricitieswinefestival.com) to Kennewick, featuring 60 different wineries.

SHOPPING

Columbia Center (1321 N. Columbia Center Blvd., 509/783-2108, 10 A.M.–9 P.M. Mon.–Sat., 11 A.M.–7 P.M. Sun.) in Kennewick is the Tri-Cities' largest shopping mall, with 100 stores including Macy's, Sears, and JCPenney.

SPORTS AND RECREATION
Cycling
The Sacajawea Heritage Trail is a 22-mile contiguous path linking Tri-Cities' parks. Kennewick's **Columbia Park** has a popular six-mile paved, nearly level path, and Richland's Riverfront Trail offers a shady seven-mile option for biking or in-line skating.

Boating
Rent pontoon boats at **Columbia Park Marina** (1776 Columbia Dr. SE, Richland, 509/783-3802).

Racing
At Kennewick's Benton-Franklin Fairgrounds, **Sundowns Horseracing Track** (E. 10th Ave., 509/582-5434) hosts quarterhorse racing in the spring and fall.

Golf
Golfers have plenty of courses to choose from in the Tri-Cities area. **Columbia Point Golf Course** (225 Columbia Pt. Dr., Richland, 509/946-0710, http://playcolumbiapoint.com, $35–45) is a municipal that doesn't look like

a municipal. The rolling, mounded fairways and water features make for a fun 18. **Canyon Lakes Golf Course** (3700 Canyon Lakes Dr. in Kennewick, 509/582-3736, www.canyonlakes golfcourse.com, $51–54) is a slope 129 from the black tees. Hole 12 has a massive, undulating 12,000-square-foot green. And **West Richland Municipal Golf Course** (4000 Fallon Dr., 509/967-2165) is a straight links-style course following the banks of the Yakima River.

Spectator Sports
The Tri-Cities is home to two professional teams. The **Tri-City Dust Devils** (509/374-2757, www.dustdevilsbaseball.com), a Colorado Rockies "A" team, play at Pasco Stadium (6200 Burden), while the **Tri-City Americans** (509/783-9999, www.amshockey.com) smack the puck in the Western Hockey League.

ACCOMMODATIONS
It's a good idea to book your lodging well ahead, especially during July when the hydroplane races attract throngs of visitors from across the Northwest.

Under $100
Travelers on a shoestring budget will surely appreciate the facilities of **The Guest House at PNNL** (620 Battelle Boulevard, Richland, 509/943-0400, www.pnl.gov/guesthouse), a somewhat under-the-radar establishment run by the Pacific Northwest National Research Laboratory to provide lodging for visiting scientists and government workers. The unique 81-room inn offers utilitarian units reminiscent of college dorms. All guests can take advantage of the grounds' courtyard, exercise room, and coin-operated laundry machines. There are several room types to choose among. A standard dorm ($35 s) comes with a single twin bed and private bath. These are clustered in groups of 6–8 rooms with shared living room, dining room, and fully equipped kitchen. Queen studios ($75 s or $85 d) are larger private set-ups with microwave, fridge, and coffeemaker—bring your own utensils. The one-bedroom apartments ($80 s or $90 d) have a separate

bedroom with desk, a living room with hide-a-bed, and a fully equipped kitchen.

If government-style quarters aren't your thing, then try **Wright's Desert Gold Motel & RV Park** (611 Columbia Park Trail in Richland, 509/627-1000 or 800/788-4653, http://wrightsdesertgold.com, $47 d). This tight and tidy motel park has an outdoor pool, hot tub, and game room.

Quality Inn (7901 W. Quinault Ave., Kennewick, 509/735-6100 or 800/205-6938, www.scinns.com, $84–94 s or d) has nice rooms, a full breakfast, a hot tub, and a sundeck.

Settled back in a residential neighborhood, **Cabin Suites** (115 N. Yelm St., Kennewick, www.cabinsuites.com, 509/374-3966, $75–95 s or d) isn't a real cabin per se, but all three rooms are alluringly decorated with rough-hewn log bed frames and plaid flannel linens. This is a private B&B, as the innkeepers don't live on-site, only coming in the morning to serve breakfast. For maximum seclusion, the whole house can be rented for $195.

$100-150

All three of the Tri-Cities are full of reasonably priced chains. One of the best values is **Hampton Inn** (486 Bradley Blvd., 509/943-4400, www.hampton-inn.com, $117 d) in Richland. This snappily decorated establishment faces the Columbia River, offering dock facilities for boaters and a pretty view for the rest of us. Do yourself a favor and plunk down an extra $20 for a room with a view. The property has a fitness center and a hot tub and offers a continental breakfast and a complimentary airport shuttle.

Another good bet is **Best Western Kennewick** (4001 W. 27th Ave., Kennewick, 509/586-1332, www.bestwestern.com/kennewick, $85–130 d), a clean and friendly property with a raft of amenities. There's an indoor pool, hot tub, sauna, and fitness center, plus a business center. Pets are welcome, and there's room outside to walk them. The hotel serves a hot breakfast buffet with French toast, biscuits and gravy, sausage, bacon, and more. Come evening time, staff sets out warm cookies. Suites

with whirlpool bath and fireplace are available for $170.

Relax to the sound of a gurgling fountain waterfall on the shady and secluded patio at **Cherry Chalet** (8101 W. 10th, Kennewick, 509/783-6406, $160 d). This modest suburban-style home is cloistered on a 20-acre cherry orchard that's close enough to Kennewick to offer easy access to restaurants and activities.

Camping

Private RV parks in the Tri-Cities area include **Columbia Mobile Village** (4815 W. Clearwater Ave., Kennewick, 509/783-3314), **Desert Gold RV Park** (611 Columbia Dr. SE, Richland, 509/627-1000, http://wrightsdesertgold.com), **Green Tree RV Park** (2200 N. 4th, Pasco, 509/547-6220) and **Trailer City Park** (7120 W. Bonnie Ave., Kennewick, 509/783-2513, wwww.tri-citiesrvpark.com, $25).

FOOD
International

Casa Chapala #1 (107 E. Columbia Dr., Kennewick, 509/582-7848) has fresh Mexican food and ultra-fresh tortillas. They also have restaurants in Pasco and Richland.

Emerald of Siam (1314 Jadwin Ave., Richland, 509/946-9328, 11:30 A.M.–2 P.M. Mon.–Fri. and 5–9 P.M. daily) creates authentic and delicious Thai food and has an inexpensive lunch buffet weekdays ($8) and a popular dinner buffet on Friday and Saturday ($14).

Mandarin House (1035 Lee Blvd., Richland, 509/943-6843, 11 A.M.–2 P.M. and 4–9 P.M. Mon.–Fri., 4–9:30 P.M. Sat., closed Sun.) has the best local Chinese food.

Located in a cozy old railroad dining car, **Monterosso's Italian Restaurant** (1026 Lee Blvd., Richland, 509/946-4525, 5–10 P.M. Mon.–Thurs., 5–10 P.M. Fri.–Sat.) simmers and stews classic Italian cuisine and nightly seafood specials. Reservations are recommended.

Steaks and Burgers

For seafood, steak, prime rib, and pasta with outside riverside seating, head to **Cedars Restaurant and Lounge** (7 Clover Island, next to the Quality Inn, 509/582-2143, 5–9 P.M. Sun.–Thurs., 5–10 P.M. Fri.–Sat.).

Probably because Yakima Valley and Columbia Basin lead the nation in hops production, the Tri-Cities have become a center of microbrewed beer. **Atomic Ale Brewpub & Eatery** (1015 Lee Blvd., Richland, 509/946-5465, www.atomicale brewpub.com, 11 A.M.–10 P.M. Mon.–Thurs., 11:30 A.M.–11 P.M. Fri.–Sat., 11 A.M.–8 P.M. Sun.) is the oldest among dozens of local microbrewers. Its beers include the appropriately named Plutonium Porter, Atomic Amber, and Half-Life Hefeweizen. The menu centers on wood-fired pizzas, though they also have steaks, seafood, and bratwurst. There's live music every Monday evening.

Kimos at Rattlesnake Mountain Brewing Company (1250 Columbia Center Blvd., Richland, 509/783-5747, www.rattlesnake mountainbrewing.com, 3–11 P.M. Mon.–Thurs., 11 A.M.–1 A.M. Fri., 9 A.M.–1 A.M. Sat., 9 A.M.–10 P.M. Sun.) is one of the nicer local places and also features outside dining along the Columbia River. Oriental wasabi chicken salad and Rattlesnake Buffalo wings attract attention on its reasonably priced menu.

Markets

Visit the **Pasco Farmers Market** (4th Ave. and Columbia St., 509/545-0738, 8 A.M.–noon Wed. and Sat. May–Nov. for local produce, sausages, fresh breads, and arts and crafts. The **Kennewick's Southridge Farmers Market** (corner of Kennewick Ave. and Benton St., 509/528-4592, http://southridgefarmersmarket. com, 4–8 P.M. Thurs., Southridge Village) is small but has a particular hometown feeling.

Adam's Place Country Gourmet (910 E. Game Farm Rd., Pasco, 509/582-8564, www.adamsplacecountrygourmet.com, 10 A.M.–6 P.M. Mon.–Fri., 10 A.M.–2 P.M. Sat., closed Sun.) is located in an apple orchard and makes all sorts of sweet confections, even chocolate-covered pizzas.

Country Mercantile (232 Crestloch Rd., 10 mi. north of Pasco, 509/545-2192, www.country mercantile.com, 7 A.M.–8 P.M. daily) has a produce market and ice-cream parlor, and provides "agricultural entertainment" in October that includes a seasonal corn-field maze, petting zoo, and pumpkin patch. It's great fun for families.

INFORMATION

Pick up all the current maps and information you need from the **Tri-Cities Visitor and Convention Bureau** (7130 W. Grandridge Blvd. in Kennewick, 509/735-8486 or 800/254-5824, www.tcrchamber.com, 8 A.M.–5 P.M. Mon.–Fri.).

GETTING THERE AND AROUND
By Bus and Train

Public transportation comes together at the **Transportation Depot** (535 N. 1st Ave.) in Pasco. Here you can catch a local bus from **Ben Franklin Transit** (509/735-5100, www .bft.org, $1, $2.75 all-day pass) for service to the three cities and the airport Monday–Saturday. **Greyhound** (509/547-3151 or 800/231-2222, www.greyhound.com) also stops here, as does **Amtrak** (509/545-1554 or 800/872-7245, www .amtrak.com), whose *Empire Builder* train provides daily service east to Spokane, Minneapolis, and Chicago, and west to Portland.

By Air

Departing from the Tri-Cities Regional Airport in Pasco are **Alaska Airlines** (800/252-7522, www.alaskaairlines.com), **Delta Air Lines** (800/221-1212, www.delta.com), and **United Express** (800/241-6522, www.ual.com).

Bergstrom Aircraft (509/547-6271) offers flightseeing trips out of the Richland airport over the Tri-Cities area for $99 for up to three people on a Cesna 172.

Tours

Columbia River Journeys (509/734-9941 or 888/486-9119, www.columbiariverjourneys .com) runs jetboat trips to Hanford Reach. As you cruise up the river, you'll see heron rookeries, curious coyotes, huge salmon beds, and the surreal Hanford reactors along the horizon.

Walla Walla

As you drive toward Walla Walla from the east, Highway 12 takes you past mile after mile of gently rolling wheat growing out of the rich chocolate-brown soil. It's enough to make Midwest farmers drool. The strip-cropped patterns of plowed and fallow land look like cresting waves, with the Blue Mountains bordering the southeast horizon. The valley enjoys a long growing season, with wheat, potatoes, asparagus, peas, alfalfa, grapes, and the famous Walla Walla sweet onions as the big money crops. Livestock and dairy products are also significant parts of the economy.

If you arrive in the pretty town of Walla Walla on a hot summer day, you'll probably wonder, at least momentarily, if you took a wrong turn somewhere and drove to New England. Walla Walla is an oasis in arid eastern Washington. Here, trees have been cultivated for decades and offer much-needed shade and visual relief from the sameness of the eastern Washington landscape.

The Lewis and Clark party passed through the Native American hunting grounds here in 1805, but the first permanent white settlement wasn't until some time later. Dr. Marcus Whitman, a doctor and Presbyterian missionary, arrived in 1836 and established a settlement he called Waiilatpu. The Cayuse, suffering from measles that Whitman could not cure and resentful of Whitman and his party's aggressive conversion techniques, massacred 15 of the settlers in 1847, including Whitman and his wife. This put a bit of a damper on local white settlement until the Treaty of 1855 reopened the region to American migration.

In 1856, Col. Edward Steptoe built **Fort Walla Walla** at Mill Creek to keep the peace. The surrounding town was later named Walla Walla, meaning "Many Waters" in the Cayuse tongue. In 1859, the city was named the county seat and has since witnessed many booms and busts, from a minor gold rush in neighboring Idaho to disastrous fires that razed the entire

© ERICKA CHICKOWSKI

log cabin at Fort Walla Walla

town to the renaissance in the local wine industry that has made the town well known today.

SIGHTS
Museums

Step back in time with a visit to the **Fort Walla Walla Museum Complex** (Dalles Military & Myra Road, 509/525-7703, www.fortwalla wallamuseum.org, 10 A.M.–5 P.M. Tues.–Sun. Apr.–Oct., $7 adults, $6 seniors and students, $3 ages 6–12, free for younger kids). This excellent museum features 15 original and re-created pioneer buildings. A 19th-century cemetery containing the bodies of both Native Americans and cavalry soldiers borders the property. A short nature trail and campground is nearby.

Visit the **Kirkman House** (214 N. Colville, 509/529-4373, www.kirkmanhousemuseum .org, 10 A.M.–4 P.M. Wed.–Sat., 1–4 P.M. Sun., $5 adults, $2 students and seniors), a redbrick mansion built in 1880 by entrepreneur William Kirkman. The ornate Italianate-style structure features a widow's walk and figurehead keystones and is on the National Register of Historic Places.

Kids will be nearly overcome with wonder and delight at the **Children's Museum of Walla Walla** (77 Wainwright Place, 509/526-

---

ONION POWER

Although wheat is the most important crop in the Walla Walla area, onions are the town's claim to fame. The famous Walla Walla sweet onions were developed from Spanish and Italian varieties first brought here in the late 19th century. These mild-flavored, juicy, large onions actually have almost no sugar, but they have only half the sulfur of other onions. And it's the sulfur that gives onions their strong bite and causes tears.

© ERICKA CHICKOWSKI

Pick up a bag of Walla Walla sweets while you're in town.

7529, www.cmwallawalla.org, 10 A.M.–5 P.M. Thurs.–Sun., $4). The tykes can jump around on stage in costume along with life-size puppets at the Enchanted Theater. The Bug Patch Party Room is full of flowers and various kinds of insects. Kids can pretend to shop at the Wee Walla Walla Harvest Market, and visit a make-believe doctor's office, Mexican restaurant, or Construction Junction. Check the website for special events planned throughout the year.

Walking Tour

Pick up a brochure from the chamber of commerce for a walking tour of the historic downtown area. Some of the sights you'll pass are the 1917 **Liberty Theatre,** built on the site of the original army fort at W. Main and Colville, and the **Dacres Hotel,** built in 1899 at W. Main and 4th. The **Reynolds-Day Building,** on Main between 1st and 2nd, was constructed in 1874. Washington's first State Constitutional Convention was held here in 1878. It's hard to miss the 10-story **Marcus Whitman Hotel,** built in 1928 at 2nd and W. Rose, the brick centerpiece of downtown. The **Baker Boyer Bank** is the oldest bank in Washington and one of the few independent banks left in the state. Its seven-story home office at the corner of Main and 2nd Streets was built in 1910 and was the town's first "skyscraper."

If you've got a kitchen and a barbecue in your hotel unit, grab a bag of sweets while in Walla Walla and wow your travel companions with the following recipe.

GRILLED AND ROASTED WALLA WALLA SWEETS WITH PINE NUT BUTTER

4 medium Walla Walla sweet onions, peeled and cut in half from top to bottom

1 tablespoon olive oil

½ cup pine nuts, toasted

3 ounces unsalted butter, softened

½ teaspoon lemon zest

½ teaspoon chopped fresh rosemary

¼ teaspoon freshly ground black pepper

¼ teaspoon salt, or to taste

⅓ cup freshly grated parmesan cheese

2 tablespoons toasted pine nuts, lemon wedges, and rosemary sprigs for garnish

1. Toast the pine nuts in a 350°F oven for 6-7 minutes, or until golden brown. Cool. Caution: pine nuts burn easily.

2. Preheat the oven to 375°F and prep an outdoor grill. Brush onions with oil and place cut side down on the preheated grill. Once grill marks form, put onions on a cookie sheet and cook in oven for another 25 minutes, or until tender. Barbecue step can be replaced by broiling – just be sure to let the oven cool once you are ready to finish cooking.

3. While onions are cooking, take roasted pine nuts and pulse them in a food processor until finely ground. Then put butter, lemon zest, rosemary, black pepper, and salt in the bowl and process until smooth. If you're traveling, you'll need to improvise: place pine nuts in a zip-top bag and crush finely with a frying pan. Place in a bowl and mix with the rest of the ingredients.

4. Spread pine nut butter over the cooked onions and put back in oven until butter is melted.

5. Serve warm, with grated parmesan and a few extra pine nuts sprinkled over them.

Recipe courtesy of the Walla Walla Sweet Onion Marketing Committee and Chef Tom Douglas, who serves this dish at Dahlia Lounge in Seattle.

Founded in 1859, **Whitman University** (www.whitman.edu) was the first higher education center in the West and is home to 1,300 students. The campus is just west of downtown Walla Walla. The tall clock tower, built in 1900, is on the National Register of Historic Places.

Big Trees and Parks

Walla Walla is famous for its tall, stately trees, a heritage from pioneer settlers who wanted a reminder of their eastern homes. A booklet, available at the chamber of commerce, describes some of the largest of these, including the 25 different individual trees among the biggest in Washington. One of the trees, a 21-foot-in-circumference catalpa on the Whitman College campus, is the largest in America. The 47-acre **Pioneer Park** (Alder St. and Division St.) contains many more state-record trees. This well-kept city park was originally a cow pasture but now includes—in addition to marvelous forested areas—an aviary, rose garden, duck pond, swimming pool, gazebo, brass cannon, and picnic tables. The design for Pioneer Park came from John C. Olmstead, creator of New York's Central Park. **Fort Walla Walla Park** is home to more tall trees, along with the Fort Walla Walla Museum. **Mountain View Cemetery** (on S. 2nd Ave. near Abbott Rd.) dates back to 1853 and is considered one of the most attractive in the state.

Farm Tours

West from Walla Walla lies farming country with a Midwestern look; this could just as well be Nebraska. Far to the southeast lie rolling tree-covered hills that rise into the Blue Mountains. A blanket of snow covers the summits till late summer.

Take a dip in a sea of purple at the **Blue Mountain Lavender Farm** (345 Short Rd., 509/529-3276, www.bluemountainlavender .com) in nearby Lowden. Owned by a French-American family, the farm was inspired by nostalgia for the extensive lavender fields in the south of France. An on-site gift shop sells dozens of luxurious items made from the local crop. Call ahead for tours.

Whitman Mission

You can get the whole story of Marcus and Narcissa Whitman's pioneer mission on the Oregon Trail at the Whitman Mission National Historic Site (28 Whitman Mission Rd., 509/529-2761, www.nps.gov/whmi), seven miles west of Walla Walla on Highway 12. None of the original buildings remain, but you can walk self-guided trails to the mission site, grave, monument, and locations of the first house, blacksmith shop, and gristmill. Cultural demonstrations—including adobe brick making, beadwork, moccasin making, and butter churning—take place on summer weekends.

Maintained by the National Park Service, the visitors center here (8 A.M.–6 P.M. daily mid-June–Labor Day, 8 A.M.–4:30 P.M. daily the rest of the year, closed Thanksgiving, Christmas, and New Year's, $3 adults, free for kids under 16) contains a diorama of the Whitman mission, plus artifacts found here and an informative exhibit about the Cayuse tribe and the sad end to the Whitmans' work.

The grounds are open till dusk year-round. Be sure to walk up the hill to the **Whitman Memorial,** a 27-foot-tall obelisk overlooking this lonely place. Come here on a late fall day with the clouds overhead, the brown grass at your feet, great blue herons on the shore of the pond, and a chilly west wind to really appreciate the peaceful wildness that both the Cayuse and the Whitmans loved.

Wallula

The tiny settlement of Wallula stands along the east shore of Lake Wallula, the Columbia River reservoir created by McNary Dam. Look for **Two Sisters,** twin basalt pillars that the Cayuse legends said were two sisters who had been turned to stone by that trickster, Coyote. A plaque in Wallula commemorates one of the earliest garrisons in the Northwest. In 1818, the Northwest Fur Company established **Fort Nez Percé** at the junction of the Walla Walla and Columbia Rivers. The fort soon became a center for fur trade in the region. Fearing Native American attacks, the company built two strong outer walls and armed the men heavily; it was soon being called the "Gibraltar of the Columbia." In 1821, the British-owned Hudson's Bay Company took over the business, later renaming it Fort Walla Walla. The fear of attacks intensified, and in 1856 the company abandoned the fort rather than risking capture. The fort's commander ordered his men to dump the black powder and shot balls into the Columbia River to keep them out of Cayuse hands. Shortly after his men abandoned the fort, American Indian warriors burned it to the ground.

Two years later a new Fort Walla Walla rose, this time as a U.S. Army military garrison farther up the river. This fort would eventually become the center around which the city of Walla Walla grew. The original fort site later grew into the town of Wallula, but in the late 1940s, construction began on the McNary Dam downstream along the Columbia River. After its completion, the old town and fort site were inundated, and the town's residents moved to higher ground.

Wineries

Walla Walla Valley is one of Washington state's eight official viticultural appellations and is best known for cabernet sauvignon, merlot, riesling, and chardonnay grapes. There are dozens of wineries in and around town. As you head close to city limits from the west, you'll encounter the very attractive **Three Rivers Winery** (5641 West Hwy. 12, 509/526-9463, www.threeriverswinery.com, 10 A.M.–5 P.M. daily). The tasting room and winery building sit on a bank overlooking the vineyard and a large grassy area with a small three-hole pitch-and-putt course. The building itself is an impressive combination of river rock, pitched roofs, and warm-red exposed wooden beams. Inside there's a river rock bar and fireplace to keep you cozy while tasting. Try the estate-grown gewürztraminer; it is superb.

Visit **Woodward Canyon Winery** (11920 W. Hwy. 12, 509/525-4129, www.woodwardcanyon.com, 10 A.M.–5 P.M. daily), about 10 miles west of town in Lowden, for a taste of top-quality chardonnay and cabernet sauvignon. The $5 tasting fee is refundable with any

purchase. **L'Ecole No. 41 Winery** (509/525-0940, www.lecole.com, 10 A.M.–5 P.M. daily), also in Lowden, specializes in semillon and merlot wines. The tasting room is an old schoolhouse—relax by doodling on the chalkboard as you sip. Tasting fees are a refundable $5.

Other notable Walla Walla wineries include the largest local winery, **Waterbrook Winery** (31 E. Main St., 509/522-1262, www.waterbrook.com, 10 A.M.–6 P.M. Sun.–Thurs, 10 A.M.–8 P.M. Fri.–Sat.).

ENTERTAINMENT AND EVENTS
The Arts

The **Walla Walla Symphony Orchestra** (26 E. Main, 509/529-8020, www.wwsymphony.com) has been performing since 1907 and is the oldest continuously performing symphony in the West. Its season runs October–May, with the special Mares 'n' Music performance falling in June.

Founded in 1944, the **Walla Walla Little Theatre** (1130 E. Sumach, 509/529-3683, www.ltww.org) is a community theater that produces four plays each season. **Harper Joy Theatre** at Whitman University (345 Boyer, 509/527-5180) also stages several student productions each year, and the local community college puts on **Outdoor Summer Musical** productions at Fort Walla Walla amphitheater each July.

Art buffs will want to visit the **Clyde and Mary Harris Gallery** (509/527-2600) at Walla Walla College, focusing on faculty, student, and regional shows. Other galleries include the **Sheehan Gallery** (509/527-5249, www.whitman.edu/sheehan) at Whitman College, home of the Davis Collection of Asian Art. The **Carnegie Art Center** (109 S. Palouse, 509/525-4270, www.carnegieart.com, 11 A.M.–4:30 P.M. Tues.–Sat., free) sits on the site of the historic 1855 Great Indian Council. Once a public library, the 1904 building is home to a pottery studio and a changing gallery of largely regional artwork.

Festivals and Events

A popular event with photographers is the

Walla Walla Balloon Stampede held in mid-May. The Northwest's signature hot-air balloon rally stages concerts, arts and crafts displays, and plenty of food to go along with the racing fun. A big **Fourth of July** at Pioneer Park is followed by the **Walla Walla Sweet Onion Harvest Festival** a week later. Labor Day weekend's **Walla Walla Frontier Days Fair & Rodeo** (509/527-3247) brings ropin', wrasslin', racin', and ridin' to the Walla Walla County Fairgrounds. In mid-September, the **Fall Harvest and Community Festival** at Fort Walla Walla Museum provides a chance to learn about pioneer life.

SPORTS AND RECREATION
Cycling
Enjoy the bike path from Cambridge Drive to Rooks Park, or from 9th and Dalles Military Road to Myra Road. For a more adventurous ride, head out scenic Old Milton Highway south of town. It's especially pretty in the fall.

Fishing
Walla Walla is a fly fisher's paradise, giving you the drop on unsuspecting trout, smallmouth bass, and the mighty steelhead. **Stone Creek Fly Fishers** (509/520-7039, http://stonecreek-flyfishers.com) teaches introductory classes for beginners, including special classes for women and children. Guide service is also available.

Swimming
Outdoor summer-only swimming pools (509/527-1099) include one in Jefferson Park (9th Ave. and Malcolm St.) and a 50-meter pool on Rees Avenue at Sumach Street.

Golf
Veteran's Memorial Golf Course (201 E. Rees Ave., 509/527-4507, http://vetsgolf.com), off Highway 12, is an 18-hole course open to the public. Greens fees are $29 for 18 holes or $16.75 for just the front nine.

ACCOMMODATIONS
Under $100
Colonial Motel (2279 E. Isaacs, 509/529-1220,

www.colonial-motel.com, $59 s or $79 d) is a rare local-family-owned motel with a nice view and a running waterfall on-site.

$100-150
For splendid semi-private downtown digs, check in at **The Wine Country Inn** (915 Alvarado Terrace, 509/386-3592, www.wallawallawine country.net, $150 d). The simply and tastefully appointed rooms offer wireless Internet access, 1930s flair, and private baths. Be sure to take advantage of the knowledge of the innkeepers, both of whom are long-time residents of the area.

$150-200
Prepare to relax hard-core when you check in to one of the three rooms at the **Inn At Blackberry Creek** (1126 Pleasant St., 509/522-5233, www.innatblackberrycreek.com, $144–239 d) Cozy rooms pay homage to artists Cézanne, Monet, and Renoir. The Inn is well located for visiting shops and historic sites.

The elegant **Marcus Whitman Hotel and Conference Center** (6 W. Rose St., 509/525-2200 or 866/826-9422, www.marcuswhitman

© ERICKA CHICKOWSKI

the lobby at Marcus Whitman Hotel

hotel.com, $169–194 s or d) first opened in 1927. After a major renovation, the 127-room hotel is once again Walla Walla's premier lodging choice, with 22 suites also available.

The **Fat Duck Inn** (527 Catherine, 509/526-3825 or 888/526-871, http://fatduckinn.com, $178–205 d) is a smartly decorated Craftsman cottage offering four suites and a gourmet breakfast. Amenities include a complimentary wine hour, with tastings of local vintages and the option of enjoying a delicious dinner right in its dining room for an additional charge. Well-behaved dogs are welcomed with prior arrangements.

$200-250
Take your pick when you stay at the **Walla Walla Inns** (123 East Main St., 509/301-1181 or 877/301-1181, www.wallawallainns.com, $115–325 s or d): stay in one of the six rooms at its historic downtown property or at the more tranquil hilltop Vineyard property. Children of all ages are welcomed here. The Inn pulls out all the stops for canine companions, too. A $100 nonrefundable pet fee gets you toys, treats, furniture, and even a crate, so your tail-wagger can pack light.

A unique lodging experience (unless you could be considered "livestock") is provided by the **Inn at Abeja** (2014 Mill Creek Rd., 509/522-1234, www.abeja.net, $245–295 d). The original outbuildings of this 100-year-old farm have been converted into tony, light-filled guest cottages and suites. The 35-acre vineyard property is the picture of country comfort. You can be proud to tell your friends you slept in a chicken coop. Reservations for popular local and winery events are filled by lottery.

Complimentary telescopes supplement the stellar accommodations at Touchet's **Cameo Heights Mansion** (1072 Oasis Rd., 509/394-0211, http//cameoheightsmansion.com, $199–249 d). The suites, a few of which have private entrances, are decorated after a variety of European, Mediterranean, and Asian styles. The rich breakfast might just convince you to stick around for the gourmet nighttime

offerings, including an optional private four-course fondue feast.

Camping
For information on hiking and camping in the Blue Mountains of Umatilla National Forest, visit the **Walla Walla Ranger Station** (1415 W. Rose St., 509/522-6290, www.fs.fed.us/r6/uma).

RVs can park and dump at **Four Seasons RV Resort** (1440 Dalles Military Rd., 509/529-6072, $28 per night or $168 for seven days), a privately run campground.

Tent campers can pitch at **Lewis and Clark Trail State Park** (509/337-6457), 26 miles northeast of Walla Walla. Standard tent sites large enough to fit RVs are available April 1–September 15. Primitive sites are open year-round. No reservations are accepted at this park.

FOOD
Cafés and Diners
Start your day at **Clarette's Restaurant** (15 S. Touchet, 509/529-3430, 6 a.m.–8 p.m. daily) for the best home-style breakfasts in Walla Walla. Also of note for lunch is **Cookie Tree Bakery & Café** (23 S. Spokane, 509/522-4826, www.cookietreebakeryandcafe.com, 7:30 a.m.–2:30 p.m. Mon.–Sat.), with homemade breads and pastries. **Blue Mountain Tavern and Casino** (2025 E. Isaacs Ave., 509/525-9941) serves excellent sandwiches for lunch and shows big-screen TV sports at night. No kids are allowed here.

Although Walla Walla has all the standard fast-food eateries (out on Wilbur and Isaacs), you'd do far better visiting **The Ice Burg** (616 W. Birch, 509/529-1793, 11:30–10 p.m. Sun.–Thurs., 11:30 a.m.–11 p.m. Fri.–Sat.). This popular drive-in makes great hamburgers and wonderful banana shakes.

International
The Walla Walla area has a rich Italian heritage, best illustrated by the sweet Walla Walla onion—developed by an Italian transplant to the area—and the tasty pasta houses in

town. A good example is **T. Maccarone's** (4 S. Colville St., 509/522-4776, www.tmaccarones.com, 11 A.M.–2 P.M. and 4–9 P.M. Mon.–Fri., 9 A.M.–2 P.M. and 4–9 P.M. Sat.–Sun.), a trendy place downtown that puts its own twist on traditional Italian fare. This is the best place in town to pair a Walla Walla red wine with antipasto.

The food isn't as good at **Lorenzo's** (1415 Plaza Way, 509/529-6333, 11 A.M.–9 P.M. daily), but it has a fun atmosphere and works well for starving students and money-minding families. It offers an all-you-can-eat buffet 11 A.M.–2:30 P.M. ($7.49) and 5–8 P.M. daily ($9.49). Kids 12 and under eat for $0.59 per year of age.

Looking for Mexican meals and great margaritas? Head to **El Sombrero's** (428 Ash St, 509/525-2598) for big portions and a bunch of big hats. **La Casita** (315 S. 9th Ave., 509/522-4941) has noteworthy pico de gallo and can accommodate large groups.

Pub Grub

Mill Creek Brewpub (11 S. Palouse St., 509/522-2440, http://millcreek-brewpub.com, 11 A.M.–11 P.M. Mon.–Sat., noon–9 P.M. Sun.) is a fun place with fresh-brewed beer on tap and pub grub from the kitchen.

Bakeries and Markets

Although Walla Walla has the big chain markets, one grocer is noteworthy: **Andy's Market** (1117 S. College Ave., 509/529-1003, closed Sat.) out in College Place. Because of the Seventh-day Adventist college nearby, this large market is almost entirely vegetarian. You'll find a few frozen meat items (but no pork), lots of frozen and canned "vegemeat" products, bulk foods, and plenty of gluten-free foods.

Not far away is **Rodger's Bakery** (166 N. College Ave., 509/522-2738) with breads, bagels, breadsticks, and hot soups. **John's Wheatland Bakery** (1828 E. Isaacs, 509/522-2253) is another excellent bake shop that uses fresh local ingredients.

INFORMATION

For local information, contact the **Walla Walla Chamber of Commerce** (29 E. Sumach, 509/525-0850 or 877/998-4748, www.wvvchamber.com, 8:30 A.M.–5 P.M. Mon.–Fri. all year, plus 9 A.M.–4 P.M. Sat.–Sun. in the summer).

GETTING THERE AND AROUND

Valley Transit (509/525-9140, www.valleytransit.com) serves the Walla Walla and College Place area Monday–Saturday. The **Greyhound depot** (509/525-9313 or 800/231-2222, www.greyhound.com) is at 315 N. 2nd Street.

Walla Walla Regional Airport is at 310 A Street and provides passenger terminals for **Alaska Airlines** (800/252-7522, www.alaskaair.com) service to Seattle and Portland. **Blue Ridge Aircraft** is the local fixed-based operator (FBO). Information is available at 509/529-4243.

www.moon.com

DESTINATIONS | ACTIVITIES | BLOGS | MAPS | BOOKS

MOON.COM is ready to help plan your next trip! Filled with fresh trip ideas and strategies, author interviews, informative travel blogs, a detailed map library, and descriptions of all the Moon guidebooks, Moon.com is all you need to get out and explore the world—or even places in your own backyard. While at Moon.com, sign up for our monthly e-newsletter for updates on new releases, travel tips, and expert advice from our on-the-go Moon authors. As always, when you travel with Moon, expect an experience that is uncommon and truly unique.

KEEP UP WITH MOON ON FACEBOOK AND TWITTER
JOIN THE MOON PHOTO GROUP ON FLICKR

MAP SYMBOLS

▭▭▭	Expressway	〖	Highlight	✗	Airfield	♿	Golf Course
·········	Primary Road	○	City/Town	✗	Airport	▯	Parking Area
▬▬▬	Secondary Road	◉	State Capital	▲	Mountain	▰	Archaeological Site
▪ ▪ ▪ ▪	Unpaved Road	❀	National Capital	✛	Unique Natural Feature	⌖	Church
-------	Trail	★	Point of Interest			⛽	Gas Station
············	Ferry	•	Accommodation	⬃	Waterfall		Glacier
⊷⊷⊷	Railroad	▼	Restaurant/Bar	▲	Park		Mangrove
▓▓▓	Pedestrian Walkway	▪	Other Location	ⓣ	Trailhead		Reef
⊪⊪⊪	Stairs	⋀	Campground	⛷	Skiing Area		Swamp

CONVERSION TABLES

°C = (°F - 32) / 1.8
°F = (°C x 1.8) + 32
1 inch = 2.54 centimeters (cm)
1 foot = 0.304 meters (m)
1 yard = 0.914 meters
1 mile = 1.6093 kilometers (km)
1 km = 0.6214 miles
1 fathom = 1.8288 m
1 chain = 20.1168 m
1 furlong = 201.168 m
1 acre = 0.4047 hectares
1 sq km = 100 hectares
1 sq mile = 2.59 square km
1 ounce = 28.35 grams
1 pound = 0.4536 kilograms
1 short ton = 0.90718 metric ton
1 short ton = 2,000 pounds
1 long ton = 1.016 metric tons
1 long ton = 2,240 pounds
1 metric ton = 1,000 kilograms
1 quart = 0.94635 liters
1 US gallon = 3.7854 liters
1 Imperial gallon = 4.5459 liters
1 nautical mile = 1.852 km

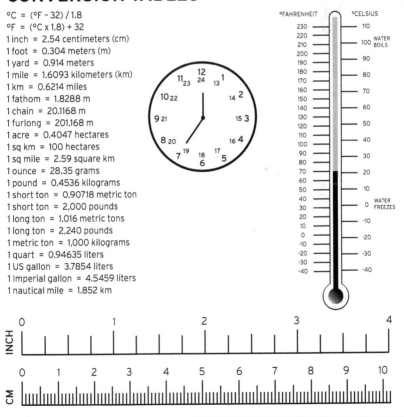

MOON SPOTLIGHT COLUMBIA RIVER GORGE

Avalon Travel
a member of the Perseus Books Group
1700 Fourth Street
Berkeley, CA 94710, USA
www.moon.com

Editor: Leah Gordon
Series Manager: Kathryn Ettinger
Copy Editor: Kim Runciman
Graphics Coordinators: Kathryn Osgood,
    Elizabeth Jang
Production Coordinator: Elizabeth Jang
Cover Designer: Elizabeth Jang
Map Editor: Kat Bennett
Cartographers: Lohnes & Wright, Kat Bennett,
    Chris Henrick

ISBN-13: 978-1-59880-763-9

Front cover photo: Columbia River Gorge © Rigucci/
Dreamstime.com
Title page photo: Vista House at Crown Point © Jit Lim/
123rf.com

Printed in the United States

ABOUT THE AUTHOR

Ericka Chickowski

When Ericka Chickowski was a kid, her parents told her she had too many recreational interests. Little did they know these would serve her well in her career as a freelance writer. Over the better half of a decade, she has covered everything from river rafting to llama trekking. Ericka's travel stories have appeared in publications such as *The Seattle Post-Intelligencer, Alaska Airlines Magazine,* and *Midwest Airlines Magazine.* She is also a respected technology journalist who has garnered awards from the Society of Professional Journalists for column, feature, and humor writing.

Ericka grew up under the shade of Washington's evergreens. She learned to appreciate the state's diverse landscape from the backseat of a minivan during family road trips. Once she learned to drive herself, her wanderlust and love for the outdoors sent her on a lifelong quest to explore the nooks and crannies of the state, from the windswept plateaus of dry Eastern Washington to the mossy rainforests of the Olympic Peninsula. In spite of her appreciation for nature, she still thinks one of the prettiest views of Mount Rainier is from Red Square at the Seattle campus of University of Washington, her alma mater.

Though Ericka settled down several years ago in a San Diego beach cottage with her husband, Paul, and her lovable mutt, Sandy, she regularly visits the trails, museums, and restaurants of her home state. Her quest to find the coolest roadside eateries, the funkiest museums, and the grandest vistas keeps her coming back home to Washington time and again.